DEVELOPING WRITERS

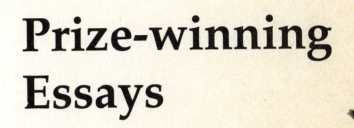

Prize-winning Essays

DEVELOPING WRITERS

Prize-winning Essays

Martin M. McKoski
Lynne C. Hahn
The University of Akron

Scott, Foresman and Company
Glenview, Illinois   Boston   London

Text of "The Dying Girl That No One Helped" by Louden Wainwright reprinted by permission.

Library of Congress Cataloging-in-Publication Data

McKoski, Martin M.
    Developing writers, prize winning essays / Martin M. McKoski,
Lynne C. Hahn.
        p.   cm.
    Includes bibliographical references and index.
    ISBN 0-673-18399-8
    1. College readers.   2. English language—Rhetoric.   3. college
prose, American.   4. American essays.   I. Hahn, Lynne C.
II. Title.
PE1417.M446   1989
808'.042—dc19

                                              88-23976
                                              CIP

Preface

Developing Writers: Prize-winning Essays is a college-level basic writing text centered around student writing. It is based on evidence from our own teaching that

- developing writers not only identify with the experiences of their peers but that the writing of their peers has a special appeal;

- successful writing by their peers is an appropriate model for instruction; and

- such writing provides evidence that developing writers' efforts are worthwhile and that success is attainable.

THE AIM AND APPROACH OF THIS BOOK

The aim of *Developing Writers: Prize-winning Essays* is simple and its approach practical: to help students develop their abilities and confidence in composing through actual practice—through *doing*. It is for this reason that the text is student-centered and employs active approaches to promote active learning.

When what is to be learned is "skill in performance, not knowledge of facts and formulas, the mode of teaching cannot be didactic," writes Mortimer Adler in *The Paideia Proposal: An Educational Manifesto* (New York: MacMillan, 1982). "Instead, it must be akin to the coaching that is done to impart athletic skills. A coach does not teach simply by telling or giving the learner a rule book to follow. A coach trains by helping the learner to *do*" (p. 27).

A class in writing, then, involves a different student-teacher relationship. It places more emphasis on the student's own engagement in the process of learning and gives a new role to the teacher who is now seen more nearly as a collaborator. Instead of attempting to impart truths, an instructor suggests and guides rather than dominates, and sets up the situation which will lead the learner herself to question, to experience, and to discover what works and what does not. The belief here is that learners learn best from self-initiated activity.

Since they both emphasize the active involvement of the writer, a process-oriented approach to writing and collaborative learning (using peer group instruction) comprise the essential activities of this text.

Writing As Process

Writing essentially involves a mutually reinforcing process: generating ideas and saying something of significance and becoming aware of readers and their needs.

In practice, this process typically begins with a **rehearsal** or pre-writing stage which refers to the thinking and writing that occur before a sustained first draft is begun. A useful rehearsal strategy effectively taps into the writer's own knowledge and liberates the flow of thought without the constraints of an early editor.

Drafting—the heart of the composing process—clarifies what a writer is trying to do for himself *as well as* the reader. It is at this stage that some resolution takes place, and something is produced and made communicable to others. Through drafting the writer communicates his intentions and views his writing through readers' eyes.

The final stage, **editing**, which is checking for surface accuracy, occurs after self-expression is accomplished and effectively communicated. Here the writer becomes proofreader and copyeditor.

It is important that students work through a process when they write, a process they determine most appropriate to themselves and the kind of writing they are doing. The process approach rejects the notion of mysterious transformations. Instead, it establishes clear intermediate objectives so that students recognize the logic inherent in the act of writing.

Segmenting writing into manageable stages also encourages feedback from peers and teachers during the process of writing instead of only afterwards, allowing writers to rethink and rewrite to bring their writing more in line with their evolving intentions.

Collaboration

The benefits of collaboration are apparent long before students enter the college classroom. As a matter of fact, probably one of the reasons that classroom collaboration is so effective is that it does, indeed, reflect reality. Through experience students and nonstudents alike come to know the value of seeking a second opinion from informed or experienced sources: peers, parents, coaches, teachers, books, or other "experts." This practical approach works particularly well in the writing classroom.

As presented in this text, collaborative activities are an integral part of the process approach and important at every stage of the writing.

Initially, "talking through" experiences is an especially effective technique for narrowing the gap between familiar, spoken communication and the more demanding, written form. For this reason, discussion has been included at the prewriting, or rehearsal, stages of the process. Relying on one's own instincts and verbal abilities when relating experiences or ideas to an interested, responsive listener facilitates the transfer of information and details when the speaker/writer begins to actually write for a reader, for she now has a guide: readers need, want, and enjoy the same kinds of information as listeners do. And if in the telling, desirable details are sometimes omitted, an involved listener can coax them forward for later inclusion in the writing.

Since a primary goal of developing writers is to acquire the perspective of readers when they write, collaborative learning is invaluable during the composing/drafting stages of the process. During this highly interactive stage, students alternately act as writers, readers, listeners, and critics. Drawing on each other's strengths, this community of writers comes to feel a sense of shared responsibility, with members contributing from their respective areas of expertise: syntax, grammar, punctuation, a strong sense of audience, or humor. It is through these activities that students internalize the writer-reader role when they compose.

An overall aim of the textbook has been to keep the classroom activities flexible. Group work can function at the teacher's discretion; that is, "groups" can mean pairs, triads, several members, or even an entire class, depending on class size, the activity, and the wishes of the instructor. Further preferences, too, will dictate whether group memberships remain constant throughout the term or whether they vary from class meeting to class meeting since, of course, there are advantages to both arrangements.

The Essays

Developing Writers, though it does not teach reading *per se*, does enhance the necessary interplay between reading and writing by actively involving its readers. The essays act as stimuli for writing assignments in the following way. Students are asked to make as many associations as possible with the various pieces as they read, whether with words, ideas, phrases, or the entire piece, virtually anything with which the reader can identify or "connect." These associations are then used as subjects for their own compositions.

Asking students to use reading in this way offers several distinct advantages. First, students can connect with the piece at any level commensurate with their abilities. Further, with this approach there is not a single, "right answer." Rather, students think about, discuss, and write about the piece from various points of view and experience as they react in their own unique ways. This, then, is an active approach that encourages active involvement with reading that is particularly accessible by virtue of both authorship and interest. Developing writers, many of whom profess not to be readers, find this a pragmatic, interesting way to bring more reading into their lives.

ACKNOWLEDGMENTS

We particularly want to thank

- our prize-winning student writers—and their teachers—from whom we learned, once again, about the significant connection between writing and one's life;

- our essay contest judges—Andrea Lunsford, Ohio State University; Donna Gorrell, University of Wisconsin—Milwaukee; Mary Jo Berger, Denver Auraria Community College—who assisted us in the enormous task of selecting the winning essays;

- our reviewers—Michael Blitz, Rutgers University; Don Barshis, Loop College; Robert Klang, De Anza College; Marcia Curtis, University of Massachusetts—Amherst; Patricia Ann Benner, Evergreen Valley College; Dennis Keen, University of Washington; Fran Zaniello, Northern Kentucky University; Gratia Murphy, Youngstown State University; Karen Greenberg, Hunter College, CUNY; Jane Lehmann, Elgin Community College; Patrick Hartwell, Indiana University of Pennsylvania—who helped us to see what needed re-seeing;

- our editors at Scott Foresman, Anne Smith, Patricia Rossi, and Carol Leon, for encouraging us to take on a project of our liking;

- our secretaries, Shirley A. McKee and Marykay Bryan, who were absolutely invaluable in the preparation of this manuscript.

Contents

Chapter 1

Prize-winning Writing: What's Appealing About It to You?

Developing Writers: Prize-winning Essays is a collection of the top twenty-two winners in a national contest held for basic writers in 1986. The essays are diverse (some are descriptions, others personal experiences, and some are paragraphs while others are essay length), but all are the products of college students like you, who were in the process of developing their writing abilities. Though there is much variety among the essays, they are all considered to be good writing.

Although readers have different ideas about what good writing is, probably most would agree that there is something about good writing that makes them want to read it, or once they have read it, they find it worthwhile or personally satisfying. For example, following are two very different pieces by prize-winning essayists:

TOM DYSER
The University of Akron (Ohio)

AT LAST, RELIEF

The clamp that Bob, my partner, and I were working with had always left me in awe of its tremendous size and clamping ability. It's nearly six feet tall, weighs a full ton, and when clamped it applies approximately twelve hundred pounds of pressure, per square inch, on anything that happens to be in its jaws. We have, on occasion, inserted a bent, half-inch thick, solid steel bar into the clamp and watched the bar straighten out as though it were made of warm plastic. After such an occasion, I commented to Bob how horrible it would be if anyone would get their hands caught in there. Hands caught in that clamp would turn to powder instantly. A year later, much to my horror, I found out exactly what it would be like. On April 10, 1984, we were setting up Press No. 1208, at B.F. Goodrich, for operation. The upper platent of the press was being equipped with a heavy pad that keeps it from burning the rubber belt after curing begins. This pad had a piece of old scrap material spliced to it. It was being drawn through the press when the scrap material broke. In an attempt to prevent the pad from slipping out of the machine, I, at the north end of the machine, pressed my weight, with both hands, on top of the pad inside the opened clamp. Bob, the operator, was at the opposite end, and was unable to see me. He wasn't aware of my hands being in the clamp. Without warning, he pulled the button which caused the clamp to close, crushing all of my fingers. Having turned my head for just a fraction of a second to look at the wall clock, I felt a pressure so great that I exploded into a scream that came from the abyss of Hell and went straight to the third floor of the shop. My eyes were as large as oranges and my mouth opened beyond its limits. The noise of stepping on popcorn while running down the theater aisle, as a small boy, came bursting into my crazed head. Every bone God put into my fingers crumbled into powder. My gloves were no protection against the savageness of its bite. Being in that clamp, for only seconds, seemed like an eternity. I thought relief would come when they opened it up, but it wasn't to be. My fingers felt as though somebody was holding them in a deep fryer. With my mind whirling, my breathing increased giving the impression of having sprinted the last fifty meters of a mile run. My speech became incessant. I repeated the Lord's Prayer over, and over, and over again, and again and again. As they were wheeling me to the elevator, my feet were moving so rapidly that they thought I was convulsing. Between the Lord's Prayer and my heavy breathing I managed to tell them to leave my feet alone, for it helped. It didn't stop the pain, but was a distraction for me. Oh God, my hands were on fire! Relief would come only when I went to surgery. Then they would put me under. The ambulance ride was swift and my incessant talking was swifter. The attendant glanced at my flattened hands but turned away. It was his first night on the job. At the emergency room a host of doctors and nurses met me, each having a specific job to perform. One put tubes in my nostrils giving me oxygen as they carted me to a room flooded with bright lights. A kindly nurse wearing a bright red sweater asked me questions about my family hoping that it would help distract my attention from the pain. "Let's get his clothes off and get him ready, Dr. Reef is on his way." "Get his wedding ring off." "Tom, we're going to take some x-rays, OK?"

"I can't get the ring off. It's imbedded in his finger." "Can I have
something to bite on. Please give me something." The kindly red
sweater reached over and gave me a wet washcloth. As soon as it touched
my lips, I began to shred it to pieces. My wife, now beside me, was
holding it in my mouth. When I looked into her eyes, I could see we were
truly made one, for her pain seemed even greater than mine. The ring
finally came off after cutting. Nothing was felt; to experience more
pain was not possible. As Dr. Reef stepped to my side and pulled back
the cover to look at the damage done, a rush of tears filled my eyes
for the first time. For such a large man he had the kindest and most
compassionate face I'd ever seen. He had a real puzzle to work with.
There were more pieces there than could be counted. With a calm and
gracious voice, he assured me that putting puzzles together was his
speciality, and was very good at it. With that my pain subsided as
they put me under for surgery.

SHARON MYERS
Cameron University (Oklahoma)

We sat across the table, so close, but yet never farther apart. Seventeen years of our lives are spread out in neat little stacks between us. He wants his freedom, he says, no responsibilities, no one to answer to or look out for. I try to accept his reasoning. After all, he has always worked so hard providing for us and I know he loves me. So many things these days could account for his attitude, his just turning fifty, his job falling apart. Perhaps retirement and a little freedom are just what he needs to put the spring in his walk and the light back into his eyes. Everything is settled so calmly and he gets on the plane to go back to Nevada. Nine days later, at 2:45 AM, I decide to give him a call, tell him I love him and see how things are going. A strange voice, definitely not belonging to the maid, answers the phone. Please God, how do I put the light back in my eyes?

ACTIVITY

Now take a few minutes, first, to reread the two student essays and then to jot down on paper or in the margins *anything* you liked about either or both of the pieces above. You might also note why. The things you indicate may be general qualities about the pieces as a whole or about specific parts or sections, whether paragraphs, individual sentences, or even words, that particularly appeal to you.

COLLABORATING

You will now share your responses with classmates or members of a group or with the entire class.

This practice of working together with your fellow students—and your instructor, of course—can help you see others' points of view, solve problems, exchange ideas, and get feedback on your own writing. Collaboration is natural and legitimate in other areas of life: getting a "second opinion" in the medical field is not only valued but urged; the hiring of corporate consultants is commonplace. If collaboration in these other, highly regarded, areas of life reflects the belief that "two heads are better than one," surely you should take advantage of it, too.

After you have shared your ideas, you might be interested in reading what students from one Basic Writing class at The University of Akron had to say about what they liked in the writing of, first, Tom Dyser.

"What I liked most about this story were the descriptions of emotions such as how the man felt when he looked into his wife's eyes and how the doctor appeared to him."

"The idea of having one's fingers liquified in a clamp is so horrifying that it necessarily holds one's attention."

"His descriptive words were enough for you to feel the pain but not too much so that it was distracting."

"I liked how he gave the exact day as to when this happened."

"You could feel the pain and hear the clamp shutting on his hand."

"The beginning of it was good too because it set the main part of the story up. You could see that something exciting was going to happen."

"It wasn't as if you would read the first part and then throw it away and say that's not going to be a good story."

"A lot has to do with the subject matter. Everyone can relate to pain."

"He did a terrific job of putting everything in the order it happened. The story was so full of sensory details you could almost feel you were there. It caused my stomach to tighten and a real feeling of sorrow came over me."

"His story makes me think."

And then Sharon Myers.

"Very focused, clings to the topic."

"The way she used words to describe the situation, not strange words, but simple words people use everyday. A lot of meaning in every sentence. Objective, very logical, and the last sentence is wonderful!"

"I like the way she wrote it. Her feelings came out in the short piece. She didn't have to write a lot to express how she felt."

"I found myself reading it twice to get what she actually was saying in each sentence because each sentence meant a lot to this paper."

"I also liked the part about 'How do I get the light back into my eyes.' That kind of hurt for me and made me think of past relationships."

"The reader must use imagination to grasp the paragraph, to picture the scenes filling in details as they apparently are happening, because the style of writing is in the present, events take place in such a sequence that it seems that everything is happening now, adding to emotional impact. It's intriguing because of this and also because things aren't directly stated. One wants to continue reading, to see if what they understand to be taking place is what actually is going on. I like the phrases--'light in eyes', etc. A lot is implied in phrases like that one. Great paragraph."

"I liked the way she constructed her story. Short and to the point. Very effective in getting her feelings across and in explaining what had led her to this. I liked the fact she left a lot of it for me to imagine and speculate about. She presented the necessary ingredients and emphasized them with one or two very effective phrases.

"I was just a little confused throughout the reading. Well, just at the end. I wasn't sure who had said what. But after analyzing it, it was made very clear."

"I could feel what she felt. Abandoned and totally crushed. Her feelings for him and concern for what he was going through only hurt herself. I imagined she was taken completely off guard, never dreaming there would be another lady in his life at all, let alone so soon after separation."

ACTIVITY

"Staying Tough" and "The Blind Chicken," which follow, are two more prize-winning essays. Again, as you read them, note in the margins or on separate paper those things that appeal to you about them. Your observations can be general overall comments or references to specific parts you find appealing.

LORRAINE FOGG
University of Northern Colorado

STAYING TOUGH

When I was a little girl, I would draw my father pictures of animals and houses. When I was done, I would run up and ask, "Do you like it, Daddy? Do you like it?" Sometimes he would be so busy he wouldn't hear me. Other times he would make such a big deal out of my Crayola picture that I felt on top of the world. As I got older, I looked for his approval in other ways, such as in my grades in school or in the boyfriends I chose. Throughout my life, I have looked for my father's approval in everything I've done.

My father died of cancer two years ago, and I still miss him very much. I miss so many things about him: his sense of humor, his smile, and his blue eyes that could look right through me. But most of all I miss talking to him. So many things have happened to me in the past few years that I would like to talk to him about. I have experienced a divorce, started school, and done a lot of growing up. I often wonder if he would approve of the things that have happened since his death. I guess I still need to know that he's proud of me and what I've done with my life.

One night I had a very strange dream that involved my father. I was at my parents' house visiting my mom and dad. My father was well and sitting in his favorite chair at the dining room table. He was wearing the baseball cap he used to always wear when he worked in his garden, and he was visiting with my boyfriend, Mark, who dad actually had never met. My father looked so happy. Suddenly, he got up from the table and went to his room. When he came out he no longer had on the baseball cap and was wearing pajamas. He was very thin and ill. His skin was yellow from a dying liver, just as it was when he was in the hospital before his death. He sat down at the table and said, "I'm going to die." I started to cry, shaking my head, not wanting to hear what he was saying. He then said, "I'm proud of you, Lori. You'll make it just fine without me. Be tough!" Then I woke up. This was the only dream I've had of my father since his death.

I have always felt that I never completely accepted my father's death. My mother and brother always felt that I would fall apart when my father died because of the special relationship that I had with him. When I was called to the hospital, in the last few days of my father's life, my mother had a priest waiting for me just in case I became too emotional. I was determined to show them that I was tough and would not fall apart. Throughout that terrible time of my father's death and funeral I was the tough one, the one that everyone leaned on. The terrible thing was that I was so busy being tough that I never got the chance to realize that my daddy was gone. Suddenly, it hit me that I had to learn to live without him.

I feel that the dream helped me to accept the fact that my father is gone. Time will also help me to deal with my loss and learn to live with it. Eventually, I feel that I will be able to think back on my father and smile, for no one can take my memories away. The dream also

made me realize that, just as I did as a little girl with my drawings,
I am still looking for my father's approval. Somehow, through this
dream I feel that I have received it.

JOE ADAMS
Los Angeles Pierce College

THE BLIND CHICKEN

The blind chicken nests alone as the other hens walk in and out of
the open coop. The blind bird sits in a corner as if she is incubating
some imaginary egg. The other hens seem to pay no attention to her
unless she gets in their way. Then they'll peck at her and walk away.

Each day I see this sightless hen's body withering away
regardless of the countless days that I spend holding a can of chicken
scratch in front of her beak. As I stand outside the coop and watch her
when she gets hungry, she goes to the free feed bucket out of habit;
even then, she can't find the bottom lip of the bucket, which holds
the feed. She will peck at the ground or hit her face on the side of the
bucket trying to get at the food.

The lack of sight keeps her down when she is hungry or thirsty; as
a result, she is losing weight and growing weaker by the day. If this
blind bird has more energy than is required for sustaining life, she
is not showing it. She doesn't go for water as often as she should, nor
is she eating as often as the other hens.

The hen's feathers are dry and falling off, as dead leaves would
fall off a dead tree, floating helplessly to the ground. I've watched
this bird that became blind from some unknown trauma go from a normal,
healthy state to a malnourished lump of feathers lying on the ground.

She went from the top of the pecking order to a helpless pecking bag
for the other hens.

 After you have read the essays and jotted down what you liked about them, take a few minutes to pull your ideas together by looking over your comments. Then freely write *a page or so*, including your thoughts about what appealed to you and why. As you write, also include any ideas you have about what you think is good about the pieces, things that you might want to include in your own writing. At this stage, just write freely, not worrying about the rules and mechanics of writing. Concentrate instead on your ideas.

COLLABORATING

After you have freely written down your ideas, share some of them with class-mates or members of a group. Then with the entire class discuss things that you seem to agree on that are appealing or good about what you have just read.

ACTIVITY

So far, all of you have read the same four essays and shared your ideas about them. Now, for this activity, choose one from the four that you especially liked or that had a particular appeal for you. With your choice in mind, jot down your reactions or responses to the following questions:

Why specifically did you choose this one?

When you read other things, what guides your choices? That is, if you could choose to read anything you want, what would you choose? Why?

What do you look for in a piece of reading?

What makes you finish something when you start it, or turns you off and keeps you from completing it? Do you think you have to finish something that you have started?

If you don't read much, why do you think that is?

Do you ever read to others? Have others ever read to you?

COLLABORATING

Share your written responses, first, with the members of your group and, then, with the entire class.

Now freely write a page or so in response to one or more of the following questions related to your discussion. Since this is not a finished piece of writing, do not worry about the rules and mechanics of writing. Concentrate instead on your ideas.

What are some of the reasons people read?

What are some of the benefits that can be derived from reading? How might reading benefit you personally?

Finally, do you think there is a connection between being a person who reads a lot and being a good writer? If so, what do you think the connection is?

COLLABORATING

When you have completed your written response, share it with the members of your group and then with your classmates.

Chapter 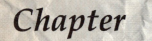 **2**

Approaches to Composing

After reading the essays in Chapter One, you had an opportunity to decide for yourself what you liked about them. You also had a chance to think about including in your own writing some of the things you found appealing. In this chapter, you will get to see a number of essays not in final form, finished and polished, but from a different angle. Here you will see essays in the making, showing the lengthy and often unpredictable process the writers took their papers through. In fact, investigation has shown that good writers rarely create successful pieces of writing in one smooth, easy step. And the prize-winning essayists in this book are no exception. To get their essays into final form as shown in Chapter Four, all the student writers developed their essays by taking their ideas through a number of stages. As you look through the early stages of the four essays that follow, you will see that this process, though differing from writer to writer, entails beginning from scratch by finding a way to get started.

ESSAY I

Lue Ann Deveny's approach to beginning her essay (her completed essay can be found on page 130) was to use a strategy called **freewriting.** By freely writing on the assignment, a description of a favorite place, she could focus her attention exclusively on what she wanted to write about and postpone until later having to think about the conventions and mechanics of writing. As you can see, she began with a very brief freewriting, which she then expanded through a second freewriting. The next step, her rough draft, is an expansion and reworking of this second freewriting. She wrote six additional drafts before she submitted her essay.

ACTIVITY

After you have read through the first three questions below, take a minute or so to scan Lue Ann's freewritings and rough draft. Then, in the space provided or on separate paper, write down your responses to the questions.

What's the first thing that catches your eye as you look through Lue Ann's process from her first freewriting through the rough draft?

Does the way it looks surprise you?

When you begin a writing assignment, does your approach resemble hers? Do your pages look like hers do?

With the following questions in mind, now take a closer look at her process, reading through each stage as well as you can. Again, write your responses to the questions in the space provided or on separate paper.

From her first freewriting, what would you say her general topic is?

Exactly how does she expand her topic in the second freewriting?

Given her second freewriting, what do you think she will write about in her rough draft? What made you think that? Were there any clues?

What seems most remarkable to you about her approach?

What is the advantage, do you think, of beginning a writing assignment by freewriting?

COLLABORATING

Now share your written responses with the members of your group or with the entire class.

First Freewriting

In the laundry room in the rear of
~~the~~ my house there is ~~a~~
a ~~small~~ square framed window. Just above my washer and dryer. The
first time I saw it it spoke to me.
Its really not that beautiful to
the average person, ~~what~~ with its white
layers of ~~white~~ crusted paint and the old fashioned
that ~~this~~ sticking ~~latch~~ turn lock ~~and its~~
always ~~tendency to~~ ~~come~~ open, this window ~~shows~~
open ~~me many things~~ tells me many
the things. It shows ~~to~~ me the pale pink
wind sky before ~~the~~ my much anticipated sunrise,

~~⬛⬛⬛⬛⬛⬛~~ Many times
it is exciting to look out ~~so~~ over the
hill toward the ^tree lined^ horizon to see the
~~furious~~ fury as a ^seething^ lines of thick ^grey^ scary clouds
bring the pungent smell of ~~the~~ rapid
rain, ~~⬛⬛⬛⬛⬛~~ approaching
my little spot.

Second Freewriting

In the laundry room of my house, ~~above~~ my iron, bleach, and my detergent and behind my dutiful washer & dryer is an old ~~~~ fashioned square framed window, and its probably wouldn't mean that much to ~~~~ the average person what with its crusty layers of white peeling paint and its ~~~~ little turning lock that always sticks. ~~~~ ~~or is blown open by the wind.~~

Its really not that beautiful

tarnished rusty squeaky

The first time I saw this little window I guess you could say it spoke to me. Many mornings I will anxiously rush to my window to see the pastel pink sky signifying my much anticipated sunrise. Many occasions it has been like having an expensive theater ticket as I look out over the endless hills toward the tree lined horizon to see the furious fury of a

Each

~~the~~ season~~s~~ holds a more beautiful view than the one before. In spring I see the black wet branches of the trees bursting with tiny pink + green buds. In summer the tree lined horizon is like a thick wavering blanket of green. In the fall everything make itself known/ colors watermelon red, lemon yellow,

Tangerine orange chestnut brown its natures painting. Winter time brings a gentle white powder to every crack and every branch of every tree.

The window view series as a picture frame for each season.

Rough Draft

Neatly tucked away

~~[crossed out]~~

In the small drab presence of a little
my laundry room in ~~[crossed out]~~
is an old fashioned, pullout, square
framed window. I think this is my
favorite spot. It stands just above
my dutiful washer and dryer and
right behind my constant (~~[crossed out]~~)
supply of laundry detergent. ~~[crossed out]~~
~~[crossed out]~~
~~[crossed out]~~ layers of white
crusted paint and ~~[crossed out]~~ a squeaky
brass turning lock, this window has
as if it has
probably witnessed other lifetimes.
To me this old relick is a picture
frame with an everchanging portrait.
~~[crossed out]~~ looke out of this window over
the steep hillside ~~[crossed out]~~ out ~~[crossed out]~~ beyond the
horizon, I see the pastel pink
sky of my much anticipated morning
sunrise. ~~[crossed out]~~ On ~~[crossed out]~~ occasions I'm
as though
just drawn to this window by the pungent
in time
? crisp smell of rain. ~~[crossed out]~~ ~~[crossed out]~~
~~[crossed out]~~ to see the seething lines of thick
black clouds as they creep over the
tree lined horizon. ~~[crossed out]~~
~~[crossed out]~~ The changing of the seasons each
through this window
have their own unique painting. Spring

means an exciting view of the wet black bark of the trees coming alive with lime green buds and my hillside ~~as~~ gently unfolds with daffodils. ~~Summer~~ ~~seems~~ peaceful quiet. a time for a thick, green, velvety blanket ~~of trees swaying~~ swaying trees and the constant buzz of the bees just outside the window. Fall is my favorite season as I look out over the hillside at fields of mustard yellow golden rod and brown crackly cattails. The trees all around are aglow with the dazzling colors of autumn, like watermelon red, lemon yellow, pumpkin orange + chestnut brown. At last my winter view is a careful dusting of every crack and crevice of ~~bare trees~~ with a fine (satiny or glistening) powder of snow.

Its funny how a laundry room window can yield such beauty. To me this is my private treasure.

ESSAY II

In the commentary following her essay on page 148 in Chapter Four, Judith DeGroat writes that "in the midst of tackling my Christmas shopping, it became apparent to me that Christmas would be an ideal topic for an essay." She began her essay, "Look What's Happened to Christmas," by using an approach different from Lue Ann's, one called **brainstorming.** She simply listed related ideas that came to mind about Christmas. These she expanded on and rearranged in individual sentences and short paragraphs called "Brainstorming Paragraphs." Her final, revised essay was the result of three additional drafts.

COLLABORATING

How many differences can you find between Judith's brainstorming and Lue Ann's freewriting approach? What are they?

What is the advantage of beginning a writing assignment as Judith has? When might brainstorming be more useful than freewriting as a way to begin? When might freewriting be more useful?

Can you tell from Judith's brainstorming list what her essay will be about?

How much alike are the brainstorming and the brainstorming paragraphs? Need they be alike?

Brainstorming
1. *Where has Christmas gone?*
2. *Designer stockings*
3. *99 gifts (per kid)*
4. *Use of credit cards*
5. *Loss of surprise*
6. *Religious aspect of Christmas*
7. *Commercialism*

8. Christmas in October!
9. Christmas caroling
10. Home baked goodies
11. Believing in Santa
12. My Christmas when young

Brainstorming Paragraphs

How sad it is that the true meaning of Christmas seems to have gotten lost in the shuffle, somewhere between Macy's and Toys'R Us.

Christmas over the last 20 years or so has been so commercial.

No one ever speaks of Christmas as being the day we celebrate the birth of Jesus Christ.

Christmas isn't anymore than a field day for shopping malls etc.

Children don't believe in Santa anymore; only Mom, Dad, Visa and Master Charge.

Grandma buys cookies and fruit and nut breads from her favorite bakery and wants Guess jeans for Christmas from the grandchildren.

How many people do you know that attend midnight mass on Christmas Eve.

Where has the element of surprise gone on Christmas day.

Nowadays, Mom takes the kiddies Christmas shopping with her. They pick out their pound puppies, gem doll and robateks or whatever. After all it's much easier to let kids choose their own presents. It saves time, eliminates guesswork and everyone's happy.

About the only tradition that hasn't changed is the Christmas carols. I predict that in the near future our Christmas carols will go something like this for instance: Jingle Bells

Rashing through the malls
To catch the sales each day,
As cheap as it may be,
Still can't afford to pay.
So over our heads well go
In debt for the rest of the year.
What fun to shop for family and
        friends
To bring them Christmas cheer.

Jingle bells, Christmas sells,
Use credit cards all the way!
Oh! What fun it is to charge
And bring home gifts today.
(repeat)

Help! It's time to wake up
America. Christmas has become
nothing more than a field day for
department stores, and most
of us have fallen into the commercial trap. We are robbing
our children of the real joy of
Christmas and the true meaning
it holds. If we can restore old
Victorian homes, trolley cars and
the Statue of Liberty etc.; then
surely we can restore Christmas
to the beautiful holiday it once
was.

ESSAY III

Kevin Larcher's essay, "My Summer Job: A Pleasant Fate," on page 140 was his response to the assigned topic on what he liked or disliked about a job he had had. He developed an **outline** as the basis of his first rough draft. For him, an outline was a way to group his ideas and give direction to his draft.

COLLABORATING

Read through Kevin's outline and rough draft as best you can. Then use the questions below to help you think about his approach to beginning his essay.

How closely does his rough draft resemble his outline?

If it differs from his outline, where and how does it differ?

Why do you think he made the changes?

What advantages are there to beginning with an outline? Are there any limitations to an outline?

What else do you notice about the rough draft?

Do you think there would be any advantage to using an outline *after* writing a rough draft rather than before? If so, what would it be?

Outline

1. My job as a carpenter in Lake Tahoe, Nev. was one of the best jobs I've ever had because of the overwhelming natural beauty of the area and the gratification of laboring at my craft.

2. Working in the beautiful area of Lake Tahoe was a privilege I'll always be thankful for.
— In the midst of the Sierra Nevada Mountain range
— Picturesque alpine lake
— Crisp, fresh mountain air
— Plentiful pine — subtle scent
— Trees blanket feet of magnificent snow-capped mountains
— Small communities dot the shoreline
— Weathered wooden boat dock, jutting out into the choppy emerald waters
— Beaches, a mass of huge granite boulders with short stretches, sand scattered aimlessly
— Night sky filled with overflowing cauldron of bright stars

3. My job as a carpenter in the midst of such a beautiful place was much too pleasurable to call work.
— At 6 in the morning the air is cold and crisp but the sun is warm and soothing

— Warm in the sun, cold in the shade

— Built very ~~expensive~~ Condominiums and chalets

— Beauty was preserved because trees and natural contours of the land were protected by law

— Condos in incline village

— Chalets were Swiss style built on hillside too steep to walk up

— Shaping and fitting plain boards and timbers to reveal symmetry and form

— From a pile of materials to a magnificent structure — almost as natural to the area as the trees

— After work my friends and I would buy a case of beer and hike to a private beach

Concl. After working for 3 summers in a row at Lake Tahoe I had to admit that all my fears were unfounded. I had enjoyed the experience more than seemed possible.

Rough Draft

All I really wanted was an easy part-time job during my summer vacation. I deserved a break. After all, since the age of 13 years old I had worked long and hard as an apprentice carpenter. Consequently, after 3 years without a vacation, I had decided that I had earned a summer of rest and relaxation. My parents, on the other hand, had their own plans for me. They persuaded me to accept a carpentry job that my Aunt Dana said was available in Nevada. My fate was sealed. I was soon having nightmarish visions of driving across the country to find myself in the middle of a dry, dusty, desert wasteland, under a bright, blistering sun, with buzzards flying overhead, waiting for me, their next meal! However, not until I arrived on the job, did I find that I would be working at Lake Tahoe. In spite of my fears, it was to be one of the best jobs I've ever had. My job sites were breathtakingly beautiful and my work was surprisingly enjoyable.

Just the opportunity of being able to soak up this incredible natural beauty of the Lake Tahoe area was merely payment enough for me. Indeed, there were times that I seemed to forget I was working. Sometimes during a break I would find a lofty perch and look out over the magnificent Tahoe Valley. I was always overcome by the awesome majesty of the scene. Encircling my view, the mighty Sierra Nevada Mountains stood proudly, protecting the fragile alpine oasis from the merciless desert sands just miles away. Tall evergreens blanketed the feet of these rocky, snow-capped mountains as if cradling the lake and fertile valley from the mountain's wind-swept harshness. Down below, surrounding the lake, the shoreline of massive granite boulders was occasionally broken with short stretches of white sand. Along the shore, small communities poked through the trees, each had their own weathered wooden boat docks, jutting out into the cold, choppy water. Beyond the docks, from the uninhabitable depths of the huge lake, the sun reflected a crystalline emerald color as brilliant and as surprising as a flawless gem. The hypnotic effects were so powerful, sometimes it took the sheer sound of hammering or an electric saw to snap me from my blissful trance.

Although I started at 6 in the morning and had a mentally and physically demanding job, I had a great time. For example, the characters I worked with in our crew were always very entertaining. Mike Swank for instance, with his rough voice and black beard looked and sounded exactly like the famous disc jockey Wolfman Jack. Another crew member, Kinook, a wild and crazy French Canadian, while riding the open back of a U-Haul truck delivering supplies, took off his clothes and started dancing around. The two ladies following closely behind seemed to enjoy the impromptu show. We were lucky we were not pulled over and arrested. Another character, which I doubt my mother would approve of, was Mike Parker. He was proud of his record. He made sure that everybody knew he was once a bouncer in a Nevada cat house. Also, that he had had various venereal diseases, more times than he could count on both hands. I stayed away from him. Not because of his past, but because he had the bad habit of shooting the nail gun at people. Similarly, everybody in the crew was unique, some maybe a bit more than others. Even though we had our fun we also took our work very seriously. Nothing has ever been more personally gratifying to me than times such as the ones when we completed a gorgeous, half-million dollar Swiss-style chalet. We knew we were a team and we knew what we had to accomplish.

Obviously, my worst fears were proved to be unfounded. The cool, crisp mountain air had cleared my mind; the hard physical labor had toned my body; and the picturesque scenery and the colorful people became treasured memories. In retrospect, I had such an incredible experience that I returned for the following next two summers.

ESSAY IV

Brent Jones' lengthy essay, "My War With Stress," on page 100 resulted from his multiple **drafting** of the first paragraph shown on page 36. Each of his *six* drafts expanded in the same way that his rough draft grew from his original paragraph. With the help and feedback of his peer group, he elaborated on his ever-expanding narrative until his war with stress was resolved.

COLLABORATING

What about Brent's approach to composing his essay is most striking to you?

What reason might explain the difference in length between the short kernel paragraph that serves now as his first paragraph, and his entire first draft?

From what you see in his draft, what would you expect the remainder of his finished essay to be about? (His completed essay, by the way, is nine typed pages.)

After reading his essay, discuss why you think he might have benefited from writing about this experience.

My War With Stress

In discussing my problem dealing with stress I feel that I must start at the very beginning of the role that the military played in my life. October 26, 1970, was what I call a milestone because that was the day I was drafted by the United States Army. Having just graduated from high school and being nineteen years old made me a prime candidate for military indoctrination and training. Basic training during the early seventies was a structured and very disciplined environment where ~~you~~ we recruits did what ~~you~~ we were told when ~~you~~ we were told to do it. The training also taught ~~you~~ us how to handle stress the military way which meant while under combat stress the job had to be done without regard for ~~your~~ our own or other human lives. But it also taught us that basic human survival was essential.

When I arrived in Viet Nam, my view of what the world was about was shattered. There I saw people living in grass huts and people starving from hunger. All the views that I grew up with, where everyone had a nice home and plenty to eat, were destroyed.

In all my wisdom I never dreamed that people could or even would want to live in poverty like the Vietnamze did. My first experience with the Vietmanze people came in Cam Rahn Bay. The second day I was there, I was placed on a trash and garbage removal detail. Our job was to go around the replacement company and collect and collect all the trash and garbage, load it on a truck, and take it to the dump. At the dump all we had to do was to let the Vietmanze unload the truck. When we arrived at the dump, we were met by a mob of hungry people who were supposed to unload the truck. The unloading started out in an orderly manner but later the people became an angry mob, grabbing for anything that was edible. We finally had to put a stop to this because we were afraid for our lives, so we fired over their heads with an M-60 machine gun to disperse the crowd. We ended up unloading the truck for the rest of the afternoon. When we returned, all of us were visably shaken from the experience since it was only our second day in the country.

The next time stress came into play was the second week after I had arrived in country. I was sent up north about twenty miles from the demilitarized zone on a fire-support base called J-Hawk. By that time I was assigned to the second of the Five o First Infantry Battalion Hundred and First Airborne Division for in-country training because I was not trained in infantry tactics. During this period of training we were only allowed three hours' sleep a night while we pulled perimeter guard. This assignment was to see how the new troops could handle the stress of combat. After three days of no sleep and not knowing if I would be alive in the morning or not, it was too much for one of the men to handle, and he fliped out; the only problem we had was that he was in control of a machine gun. We finally got him stopped after, he ran out of ammunition.

The next night we were assigned to pull perimeter guard again. Everything was going fine until about one-o-clock in the morning, when I noticed that

there was a dead silence in the jungle—
no bird or insect noises. I heard
what sounded like a jet flying over
head, but then the jet engine stopped.
The next thing I heard was someone
yelling, "Incoming!" From where I was
I turned around and saw the biggest
explosion I have ever seen. The first
122-millimeter rocket hit our ammunition
dump and there was shrapnel flying
everywhere. For about the next two hours,
the rockets kept exploding on the
compound. When the rockets stopped, we
had about twenty minutes which seemed
like hours before the North Vietnamese Army
attack started.

I was in the guard tower about
twenty feet from the wire. As I was
looking out acrossed the bunker line
through a starlight scope, I saw the
enemy troops approaching. I then got
on the radio and directed the 81-millimeter
mortar platoon to fire illumination and
high explosive rounds to fall about a
kilometer in front of the bunker line
getting ready for the attack. When our
first mortar exploded, it was like
Pandora's Box; the enemy had started
rushing the wire, screaming and yelling as

they ran toward us. We then waited for the enemy to get close before we opened up with our weapons.

When we finally got the order to fire, the whole bunker line lit up as bright as daylight, red and tracer rounds were flying everywhere; explosion after explosion went off until one of the enemy's mortar rounds hit the tower where I was. After that I don't remember much of what happened. All I remember is waking up in the unit hospital in Cam Rahn Bay about two weeks later. To this day, I don't remember what happened, but all I know is that I was awarded the Silver Star, Vietnamese Cross of Galantry with Palm and the Purple Heart. Basically the Italian stated that I helped with the medical evacuation of the wounded while being wounded myself, without regard for my own life. In the next few months I discovered what war was all about. I became a paid killer with no feelings for right or wrong. I just went out day after day not knowing whether or not I would come back from the mission.

After about four months, I began to enjoy the killing and the adrenalin high I would get from being in the jungle, not knowing what to expect next. Sometimes I would go out of my way to volunteer for crazy missions like being a door gunner on a chopper— anything to get back into action and get that addicting high. I became an emotional refrigrator, not feeling death or caring about anyone or anything (I was) anymore. An empty void with nothing inside of me. I remember when my best friend Rich was killed. All I could do was stare at his lifeless shell of a body. I felt nothing, no remorse or even a sense of loss. In other words, I became a zombie of an empopular war.

Two months before I came home, all the fear and parnoid returned. Was I going to be the last sucker to die in this God-forsaken place? I found myself watching every move I made, watching my front and my back and making sure no one was going to kill me. Even during the rocket and mortar attacks I was the first person in the trenches.

Finally the day came to go home. I remember I recieved the word from the captain while we were doing a search and destroy mission outside the provincal capital of Hue. It was nine in the morning on October 25, 1972. I backed my gear and borded a plane bound for Travis ~~Airforce bace~~ Air Force Base outside of ~~San Francisco~~ San Francisco. Little did I know, eight hours later I would be entering a different type of war, one which I am still fighting: one within myself that I probly be fighting for the rest of my life.

COLLABORATING

As a way of summing up what you have just read and discussed, you might now consider with your classmates the similarities and differences between your approach to beginning and developing a paper and those used by the four student essayists. Specifically,

> When you are asked to write, how do you go about doing it? Do you work through stages?

> How do you start a piece of writing? How do you find out what you want to say?

> Would you rather find your own subject or have your teacher give you one? Why?

> Do you ever write more than one draft? If so, why? If not, why not?

You have read and discussed several essays from a reader's perspective and had a behind-the-scene look from a writer's perspective at the processes that some of the prize-winning essayists used in composing their essays. You also have considered with your classmates your own writing process or habits. Now, using the questions below as a guide, think about and discuss your feelings and attitudes about writing. It may be helpful to write your responses before sharing them with your classmates.

> What kind of writing do you usually do? What kind of writing do you prefer to do? Do you ever write anything outside of school? Do you write letters, for instance?

> Have you ever written anything you especially liked? What did you like about it?

> What do you dislike about writing? What's hardest about writing to you? What's easiest?

> Have your feelings about your writing changed over the years? If so, why?

Do you like other people to read your writing? Do you like others to critique your work?

How have your teachers responded to your writing?

How do you feel when corrected papers are returned to you?

Do you ever ask for advice when you write? What kind of advice? Whom have you asked?

Do you proofread your writing? Do you worry about correctness?

Do you ever read your writing aloud to yourself? What does this accomplish?

Have you ever read your writing aloud to others? Were there any advantages to this?

How do you get into the frame of mind to write?

Have you ever used writing to solve a problem?

As a means of pulling together your ideas and to actually practice the strategies for beginning a paper, you will try a couple on your own, ones you have seen used by the four student essayists. Whichever you choose, think of them primarily as *rehearsals* or writing in its early stages.

REHEARSAL STRATEGIES

Freewriting/Drafting

You may have noticed that Lue Ann's freewriting and Brent's drafting had some similarities. Both students already had rough ideas of what they wanted to say and so began by actually writing out their ideas. But Lue Ann's approach, unlike Brent's, allowed her to write without being concerned with sentence structure and punctuation.

Freewriting is also a good way to find out what is on your mind when you do *not* have a direction or rough idea on a topic. Then it becomes a way to explore a topic to see what you think and feel about it. The form this kind of freewriting takes is different even from Lue Ann's. It may appear as a random series of very loosely related ideas since you are mainly searching, actually "thinking on paper."

Whether you are freewriting or drafting, it is helpful to try to get as many of your ideas as possible on paper. In other words, the more material you have to work with the better. You can always eliminate information later.

You may respond to one or two of the questions about your feelings and attitudes about writing from the list on pages 43 and 44 by either freewriting or drafting. Whichever strategy you choose, remember this is practice, not a finished paper to hand in, so do not be overly concerned with organization, completeness, or correctness.

Brainstorming/Outlining

Judith's approach, brainstorming, was to begin by quickly listing as many related ideas as she could come up with on her general topic. She did this to see what she knew about the topic and which of her ideas she might consider including in a draft.

To brainstorm, write out your general topic at the top of a blank page, then list from top to bottom any words or phrases that relate to the subject.

Outlining, a strategy of loosely grouping ideas, helped Kevin explore his topic and give some direction to his thoughts. His outline is a rough sketch of what the paragraphs of his future essay might include. Your outline, like Kevin's, need not be formal in any sense, so you may group ideas in any way that works for you.

Here you may use either brainstorming or outlining to think about or to give some direction to your thoughts on the following general topic: particular experiences that helped shape your feelings or attitudes about writing. By using the various rehearsal strategies, you now have the means for getting started on a paper. In Chapter Three you will discover ways to shape rehearsal writing into a completed, finished product.

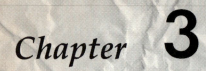

Chapter **3**

Composing

This chapter provides the basic model of the process you will use to develop any number of finished pieces of writing. It will guide you through each stage of the composing process, beginning with reading and discussion with classmates, all the way to the final development of your ideas.

The topics you select to write on will all come from your own unique reactions to and associations with the readings in Chapter Four. In other words, *you* will decide just what it is you want to write and how you choose to write it. Writing may be used either as a way of confirming what you know and feel, or as a way of exploring and discovering something new about yourself. You also will practice successfully meeting the needs of readers when you write, which includes using the conventions of writing.

The first part of this chapter shows in detail the actual evolution and development of one of the prize-winning essays, "Hidden Bitterness" by Steve Shaver. Steve's running commentary on each step in the writing of his paper is integrated with the essay to show his thoughts and feelings about the piece as it developed. You might be interested in first reading through the various stages of Steve's essay and his commentary as a preview or general guide for the process you will later use when developing your own ideas in writing.

STEVE SHAVER'S ANALYSIS OF THE WRITING PROCESS FOR HIS PRIZE-WINNING ESSAY, "HIDDEN BITTERNESS"

The main focus of my paper, "Hidden Bitterness," materialized after hearing a story from our textbook read to us by my Basic Writing teacher. The story "The Dying Girl That No One Helped," written by Loudon Wainwright in 1964, was a gut-wrenching event involving a young lady who was brutally stabbed to death in the middle of the street practically on her own doorstep while walking home to her apartment one night in New York City. Actually that was not the worst part since there were thirty-eight witnesses who admitted seeing the crime without doing a damned thing about it. In her last breaths on earth she even went as far as singling out one person, a neighbor, and called him by name in a cry for help, but instead of helping he quietly shut the blinds and went to bed, not wanting to become involved.

The Dying Girl That No One Helped
by Loudon Wainwright

The story is simple and brutal. As she arrived home in the early morning darkness, Kitty Genovese, a decent, pretty young woman of 28, was stalked through the streets close to her Kew Gardens apartment and stabbed again and again by a man who had followed her home and who took almost a half hour to kill her. During that bloody little eternity, according to an extraordinary account published in the New York Times, Kitty screamed and cried repeatedly for help. Her entreaties were unequivocal. "Oh my God!" Minutes later, she screamed, "I'm dying! I'm dying!"

The reason the murderer's actions and his victim's calls are so documented is that police were able to find 38 of Kitty's neighbors who admitted they witnessed the awful event. They heard the screams and most understood her cry for help. Peeking out their windows, many saw enough of the killer to provide a good description of his appearance and clothing. A few saw him strike Kitty, and more saw her staggering down the sidewalk after she had been stabbed twice and was looking for a place to hide. One especially sharp-eyed person was able to report that the murderer was sucking his finger as he left the scene; he had cut himself during the attack. Another witness has the awful distinction of being the only person Kitty Genovese recognized in the audience taking in her final moments.

No one really helped Kitty at all. Only one person shouted at the killer ("Let that girl alone!"), and the one phone call that was finally made to the police was placed after the murderer had got in his car and driven off. For the most part the witnesses, crouching in darkened windows like watchers of a Late Show, looked on until the play had passed beyond their view. Then they went back to bed.

Not all of these people, it must be said, understood they were watching a murder. Some thought they were looking on at a lovers' quarrel; others saw or heard so very little that they could not have reached any conclusion about the disturbance. Even if one of her neighbors had called the police promptly, it cannot be definitely stated that Kitty would have survived. But that is quite beside the point. The fact is that no one, even those who were sure something was terribly wrong, felt moved enough to act. There is, of course, no law against not being helpful.

"You know what this man told us after we caught him?" [Police Lieutenant] Jacobs asked. "He said he figured nobody would do anything to help. He heard the windows go up and saw the lights go on. He just retreated for a while and when things quieted down, he came back to finish the job."

Later, in one of the apartment houses, a witness to part of Kitty Genovese's murder talked. His comments—agonized, contradictory, guilt-ridden, self-excusing—indicate the price in bad conscience he and his neighbors are now paying. "I feel terrible about it," he said. "The thing keeps coming back in my mind. You just don't want to get involved. They might have picked me up as a suspect if I'd bounced right out there. I was getting ready, but my wife stopped me. She didn't want to be a hero's widow. I woke up about the third scream. I pulled the blind so hard it came off the window. The girl was on her knees struggling to get up. I didn't know if she was drunk or what. I never saw the man. She staggered a little when she walked, like she had a few drinks in her. I forgot the screen was there and I almost put my head through it trying to get a better look. I could see people with their heads out and hear windows going up and down all along the street."

The man walked to the window and looked down at the sidewalk. He was plainly depressed and disappointed at his own failure. "Every time I look out here now," he said, "it's like looking out at a nightmare. How could so many of us have had the same idea that we didn't need to do anything about? But that's not all that's wrong." Now he sounded betrayed and he told us what was really eating him. Those 38 witnesses had, at least, talked to the police after the murder. The man pointed to a nearby building. "There are people over there who saw everything," he said. "And there hasn't been a peep out of them yet. Not one peep."

On the scene a few days after the killer had been caught and had confessed, . . . Jacobs discussed the investigation. "The word we kept hearing from the witnesses later was 'involved,'" Jacobs said. A dark-haired, thoughtful man, he was standing on the sidewalk next to two fist-sized, dark-grey blotches on the cement. These were Kitty's bloodstains and it was there that the killer first stabbed her. "People told us they just didn't want to get involved," Jacobs said to me. "They don't want to be questioned or have to go to court." He pointed to an apartment house directly across the quiet street. "They looked down at this thing," he went on, "from four different floors of that building." Jacobs indicated the long, two-story building immediately next to him. A row of stores took up the ground floor; there were apartments on the upper floor. "Kitty lived in one of them," Jacobs said. "People were sitting right on top of the crime." He moved his arm in a gesture that included all the buildings. "It's a nice neighborhood, isn't it?" he went on. "Doesn't look like a jungle. Good, solid people. We don't expect anybody to come out into the street and fight this kind of bum. All we want is a phone call. We don't even need to know who's making it."

Due to my upbringing in the country I found it hard to believe that people could just stand around and watch something such as they did, because you can always count on your neighbors to help in the country, at least I can.

I was freewriting my thoughts and reactions to the story as it was being read to us.

Freewriting

I think the helpful attitude toward other people still exists out in the country where people aren't exposed to crime as much as city people they see it on the news and in the newspapers but it doesn't happen in front of their house or even in their neighborhoods (if thats what you want to call them) like people in cities. About the most violence they see in the country is a big pig rooting the smaller pigs away from the feed bin but people are constantly seeing or hearing about crime and violence because it happens so frequently around then they can't stay away from it and maybe thats why a lot more violence happens in the city as well as the fact that many cities may be overpopulated and the people feel other people are invading on their space so they deal with it in ways that sometimes are very harsh and many time irreversible to correct.

After freewriting for a few minutes about what we had just heard, we started a class discussion to talk over our various viewpoints. To my astonishment and disbelief I realized the majority of the people in the classroom, mostly people from the city, said they would probably react in the same manner as did the people in the story, feeling they would end up in trouble themselves for trying to help. One woman in the class was raised in the Bahamas, and she said she could go out on any given night and sit on her balcony and watch crime, although it was not as brutal, but she made it sound like it was a good form of entertainment, which gave me a very sickening feeling inside.

I began freely writing a draft of my original reaction of pure disbelief to the way the witnesses reacted. The paper was full of feelings simply stating that where I come from people would be more apt to help instead of just stand around and watch. I tried to include some statements my classmates gave for not helping; nevertheless, I found that part very hard to do, especially since I did not agree with them.

Draft 1

Being raised in the country I can see a big contrast in the way city dwellers and country folk react when it comes time to help another human being who is in need of help.

Country folk are more willing to at least try to help someone in need for the main reason that they seem closer to their neighbors because of the fact that they know them or try to get to know them. They dont feel strict limitations of valuable space that the city people feel even though country folks are exposed to the same amount of violence due to media coverage. The stone etched impression of seeing it first hand is not there in many cases which in my opinion is why many people are afraid to help someone else for fear of ending up being hurt or in trouble themselves, and another reason is city life style and general pace is so much faster compared to the slow day by day attitude of the country it is understandable when a person has to spend 45 minutes getting out of downtown of big city U.S.A. Why he would not want to stop and help someone off the highway with a flat tire because they're more than likely got dinner and theater reservations for the evening or something planned but on the other hand the country folk are pretty much on the same schedule all the time so if they stop to help someone the only inconvenience it would cause might be a short delay in starting to milk or something to that effect but it wouldn't hurt their schedule all that much.

Then, I sat back to analyze what I had written. It just didn't look right to me, for I was trying to write both sides of the story, and they were clashing, simply because I could not sit around and watch something like that happen. Naturally, it was difficult for me to write. I had to write my side and/or viewpoints of the story since they were the only ones I could give an honest opinion about. About all I can say about this early draft is that it was all mine. It showed feelings that could come only from my head. (What was missing were the examples to back up the feelings.)

Draft 2

Being raised in the country then moving to the city to go to school I can see a huge contrast in the way city dwellers and country folks react when it comes time to help another human being who is in need of help in some form or another.

It's not that city folks are mean and hateful or anything like that. But the majority of them are on such a tight schedule that they don't take time to try to understand people or to see that all people have at least a little bit of good in them. I can see why people get the I don't give a damn attitude from the city, because of such a fast pace that city life presents. With traffic jams to and from work everyday to all the people in there apartment buildings in which they don't take the time to get to know everyone is just out there doing there thing and they won't bother anyone unless someone bothers them.

But in the country on the other hand the pace is much slower and easy going. People know there neighbors and if someone new moves into the neighborhood they like to get to know them and make them feel welcome. Although there are some things that must be done regularly in the country such as milking cows or feeding animals but there is time to talk to your neighbor at the same time it just seems to me that country people have more time to spend to help someone they know or even a stranger.

The next step involved analyzing my latest draft, and to my surprise, because of a helpful hint from my teacher, I realized no matter how many feelings you tell about your paper, they're not worth a damn if you can't show some examples as well. When you construct the feelings and examples, they must be put together in such a way to show the reader a vivid picture almost as clear as a built-in camera.

In the following step the pieces finally started to come together. As I was writing a third draft, I mysteriously remembered an incident which I had been involved in only about two weeks earlier that I had completely forgotten to my great disbelief. Once I recalled the scene, the rest was easy since the picture was vivid in my mind once more. All I did was copy down the details and blend them in with my feelings.

Draft 3

I was born and raised in the country and I am presently living in Akron while attending college and it is sometimes difficult adjusting from corn fields and dirt roads to towering skyscrapers and four lane roads through town but the hardest thing I have found trouble adjusting to so far is the hidden bitterness in many of the people you see walking around please don't get me wrong I'm not saying anyone who lives in a city is heartless and cold due to the media coverage because it seems like all you here on the news anymore is bad and that naturally makes people a little leery of there fellow human beings. But what has a bigger frightening impact on a person is seeing the crimes they will put on the news first hand which makes people even more cautious they don't know who they can trust. For instance my roommate and I were downtown in the cascade plaza just the other day we were just walking around looking in the courtyard and we decided to leave and were walking toward the street and we saw a teenage boy riding a motor-cross bicycle on the crowded lunch hour street when he approached an elderly woman pulling a little cart behind her full of groceries and other items he closed down and followed her for a minute while my roommate and I were watching all of this from a distance of two feet we thought he was going to ride by and steal something from one of her bags; consequently, he did something worse he backed away from her a little bit and produced a cunning grin and look of determination on his face he picked up speed and as he went by the lady he kicked the cart with his left foot knocking it and the old woman over with a thud as this poor old lady's groceries rolled every where and the little bastard rode away laughing asking the old woman if it was her first day on her new legs. I thought that was terrible but what I saw next almost got to the point of embarrassing me to be a member of the human race no one stopped to help the woman there were people practically tripping over this poor old lady by the time we got over to her she was getting to her feet I put my hand under her shoulder to help her up and she was very upset because she thought I was going to hurt her or rob her or something while I was assuring her that all we wanted to do was help her and make sure she was all right my roommate, Steve Herbert was picking up groceries that people had kicked all over the place I can still see the Campbell's chicken noodle soup can rolling down the street that day was a first for both myself and the old lady it was a first for her because this said it was the first time in a long time that she can remember someone other than a family member wanting to help her without wanting something in return and it was a first for me because I had never been in downtown Akron before and to be honest I was not impressed.

The way our class is run we get a chance to help each other with our papers which at times can be more helpful than the teacher because you get a wider more varied viewpoint of your paper.

When we feel our drafts are completed, the class splits into two or three groups and each person reads his/her paper aloud which acts as a good sign as to how good your paper really is. No matter how good your paper sounds to you personally, a group of other people will undoubtedly find something missing whether it be details or even a focus and many times they'll find things that take away from the focus, things that should be deleted. For example, my classmates found some questions that were left unanswered to them as well as some details left out. One question I left without an answer was "Why were you at the Cascade Plaza in the first place?" They also felt that I could have given more descriptive details about the boy and the old lady as well. Last but not least my paper did not show how I got the old lady to settle down and realize all I wanted to do was help her. All I can say about this procedure is that you will no doubt end up with a much better paper.

After I combine all the above steps which includes adding or deleting information according to the class response in my final paper—and simply rely on my ears to aid me in what sounds clear as well as unclear and needs to be changed—I then go back to punctuate the paper. I found this step to suit me the best because punctuation is a downfall of mine so I need to focus my attention completely on that area when it's time. I do so by starting from the top of the paper and reading it aloud to hear how it sounds as I put in the punctuation where I think it is needed. After repeating the procedure several times I go to the very end of the paper, find the last punctuation mark, and start reading the paper from the last sentence. This allows me to maintain direct attention on each sentence not allowing me to get caught up in the story itself as I often find myself doing if I read it from the beginning.

By reading aloud I can also hear both mechanical and grammatical errors.

Steve's final draft included his classmates' suggestions for change, and appropriate punctuation. This draft, which follows, has his additional corrections and changes superimposed on it.

ADDITIONAL CHANGES AND ALTERATIONS DONE ON THE FINAL DRAFT

Final Draft

1 ~~The Cornfield Kid Rides Again~~ _Hidden Bitterness_

2 I was born and raised in the country, ~~but~~ I am presently living in Akron Ohio while attending college. It is sometimes difficult adjusting from corn fields and dirt roads to towering skyscrapers and four lane highways through town. But the hardest thing I have found trouble adjusting to so far is the hidden bitterness in many of the people walking on the streets. I think the media has a lot to do with why people are sometimes afraid of their fellow human beings, because all they like to talk about on the news anymore are all the bad things people are doing which is bound to make people leery. But ~~what makes a~~ _what really_

3 _left an indelible impression with me was seeing such an act of_ ~~guy even more skeptical is seeing such a crime first hand which in~~ _violence in person with my own two eyes._ ~~turn leaves a indelible impression~~ My roommate and I were downtown

4 in the Cascade Plaza. _on a gloomy, dreary day in early fall._ After paying our gas bill we were walking around in the courtyard minding our own business. Just as we were heading to

5 our car which was parked on main street ~~we saw~~ _our attention was focused on_ a boy who looked to be in

6 7 his teens, wearing a tattered leather coat that ~~was~~ _looked to be_ about three sizes _The boy was_ too big, a pair of worn out "nike" high topps, and a holey pair of

8 "levis". He was _skillfully_ riding a red motor-cross bicycle on the crowded

9 lunch hour street ~~when~~ _as_ he approached an elderly woman. She appeared

10 to be no more than a bag lady who was wearing very _old_ worn-out red tennis shoes, a coat that looked like an army jacket that had been through a

11 war, and a knit hat which was pulled down over her ears only ~~showing~~ _revealing_ her dirty face. She was pulling a little cart which was full of

1 *Title*

After studying the first title "The Cornfield Kid Rides Again," it sounded as if I put on a cape or something and flew all over America, from city to city, swooping down on mean, hateful city people to play the heroic, redneck farmer bit and punish all people who did not tip their hats and bellow out a hefty "how-do" to each other as they passed on the sidewalk. That was not the idea of the paper at all, nor is that my attitude toward people in the city. I simply wanted to show that I personally cannot just stand by and watch when someone is in need of help, let alone practically trip over them. That is when I thought of "Hidden Bitterness" because deep down inside, all the people that walked over this poor old lady had something telling them "Don't stop, don't get involved."

2 *"And" to "But"*

Simply a word choice that shows a difference and/or contrast in my surroundings.

3 *Getting rid of "skeptical"*

After looking at this sentence, it sounded as if I was used to seeing situations like this, which I wasn't.

4 The addition of a couple of descriptive words to help show the scene a little better.

5 *""We saw" to "our attention was focused."*

By this I mean we saw a lot of things that day, but at that particular time our attention was focused on the boy on the bicycle.

6 Simply broke up the sentence in order to put more emphasis on his appearance.

7 *Word choice*

I couldn't prove that the coat was three sizes too big, it just *looked* three sizes too big.

8 *"Skillfully"*

Added it to better describe how he was riding the bike through the crowd.

9 *"When" to "as"*

Because he was riding the bike this was *as* he approached her, and he did something else *when* he got to her.

10 *"Old"*

Just more description to shoes.

11 *"Showing" to "revealing"*

I made this word change because of the way she wore her clothes, her face was the only thing that was revealed ("showing" just did not fit).

groceries that could very well have been all she owned. The boy

12 followed the lady for a couple of minutes suddenly he produced a

cunning grin and a look of determination on his face. Then he picked *gradually*

up speed, gracefully dodging people as he approached the lady,

kicking the cart with his left foot knocking it and the old lady over

with a thud. As this poor old lady's groceries rolled everywhere,

that little bastard rode away laughing, yelling back at her to ask if

it was her first day on new legs. As if that wasn't bad enough there

13 were people practically tripping over this poor old woman ~~due to the~~ *as she lay helpless*

on the ground, but
~~fact that~~ no one ~~wanted to~~ stop and help. By the time we got over to *would* *her*

her, she was trying to get up looking like a new born fawn, trying to

get to her feet on wobbly legs. I put my hand under her shoulder to help

her to her feet, and she instantly went into a panic stricken rage

because she was afraid that I was going to rob her. While assuring her

a little bit,
14 that all we wanted to do was help, I got her to sit on a bench and relax
a
As my roommate, Steve Herbert, was picking up the groceries that

15 people had kicked all over the place, I can still see the Campbell's

(new paragraph)
16 soup can rolling down the street. That day was a first for myself and

Jean, the old lady. It was a first for Jean because she said it was the

first time in many years that she can remember someone other than a

family member wanting to help her without wanting something in

return. It was also a first for me because I had never been in downtown

Akron before and to be honest I was not impressed.

12 Broke up sentence to put more emphasis on the look he produced.

13 Added these words to better show her position and the result of the boy's kick.

14 I combined the two sentences to show that the action was taking place simultaneously.

15 I separated these sentences because the soup can rolling down the street, to me, was important enough, for it shows a picture and makes the whole story that much more vivid and brings it to life, mainly because that little soup can was an important part of Jean's life and there were people actually watching it roll away.

16 *Separation of paragraph*

I separated the ending from the main body of the paper for the simple reason that I felt it important to talk about these first time experiences that happened to us simultaneously. And it was also a good way for me to stick in my opinion of this whole experience.

WRITING ABOUT READING

An excellent source of potential topics for writing is the group of prize-winning essays in Chapter Four. Your own unique reactions or responses to the various pieces will form the basis for any number of writing assignments.

Because of our different life experiences and individual preferences, we all tend to see things—even the same things—in our own unique ways, and so a piece of reading will mean different things to different people.

Although you as a reader may respond differently from another reader to the same piece, you will undoubtedly identify or associate with something, whether it is the entire piece or individual words, phrases, or ideas. Identifying with something in reading, however, does not necessarily mean you have had similar experiences; it can, in fact, mean just the opposite.

With the variety of prize-winning essays provided, there are a number that are bound to interest you because you can relate to them in some way—either to something you particularly want to think through, or learn more about, or have a special feeling for.

The writing process you will use in response to the essays is similar to the one used by Steve Shaver, whose essay, "Hidden Bitterness," began with an association with something he read, the piece on Kitty Genovese. Through a series of freewritings and drafts, he gradually brought his paper in line with his intentions. The point is that since most writers—including the prize-winning essayists—do not usually know exactly what they want to say or how to say it before they write, they need to explore and *gradually* discover their content and the form it will take.

Although your process may vary from Steve's in some way, this approach might prove especially useful to you because it segments writing about something you have read into manageable stages so that you can concentrate on one step at a time: reading, rehearsing, multiple-drafting, and then editing.

What follows are the activities that will lead you through this process.

I. READING

Just as you associate, identify, or connect when watching a movie or television show—even if only with individual scenes—you will make a number of connections when you read. These associations will be ones that will most likely remind you of incidents from your own life, either past experiences or your personal way of viewing things. The associations you make may be unrelated to one another and only indirectly related to what you are reading. They may relate to the piece as a whole or perhaps to smaller segments, even ideas brought to mind by individual words or phrases. Some of the associations you make may be about incidents and ideas you want to explore and may lead to potential writing topics. The more associations or connections you make, the better your chances are of increasing your options and testing new possibilities for writing.

As you read one of the essays in Chapter Four, either from the first section "Intense Personal Experiences," or one assigned by your instructor, check off, circle, or underline wherever you identify or associate with the writer or whatever strikes you as particularly significant. It may be a shared experience or understanding or even disagreement. It also might be a good idea to write in the margins whatever reactions or responses you have as you read.

The following illustrates how two students in a Basic Writing class at The University of Akron used these directions to respond to Lorraine Fogg's "Staying Tough." Both students' responses and their associations, which are underlined, are included on the same copy. The comments of Student #1 are in the left-hand margin, and those of Student #2 in the right-hand margin.

Lorraine Fogg

STAYING TOUGH

When I was a little girl, I would draw my father pictures of animals and houses. When I was done, I would run up and ask, "Do you like it, Daddy? Do you like it?" Sometimes he would be so busy he wouldn't hear me. Other times he would make such a big deal out of my Crayola picture that I felt on top of the world. As I got older, I looked for his approval in other ways, such as in my grades in school or in the boyfriends I chose. Throughout my life, I have looked for my father's approval in everything I've done.

Draw many things for parents

Grew up on a farm type home

would always show him my pictures at dinner.

My father died of cancer two years ago, and I still miss him very much. I miss so many things about him: his sense of humor, his smile, and his blue eyes that could look right through me. But most of all I miss talking to him. So many things have happened to me in the past few years that I would like to talk to him about. I have experienced a divorce, started school, and done a lot of growing up. I often wonder if he would approve of the things that have happened since his death. I guess I still need to know that he's proud of me and what I've done with my life.

One night I had a very strange dream that involved my father. I was at my parents' house visiting my mom and dad. My father was well and sitting in his favorite chair at the dining room table. He was wearing the baseball cap he used to always wear when he worked in his garden, and he was visiting with my boyfriend, Mark, who dad actually never met. My father looked so happy. Suddenly, he got up from the table and went to his room. When he came out he no longer had on the baseball cap and was wearing pajamas. He was very thin and ill. His skin was yellow from a dying liver, just as it was when he was in the hospital before his death. He sat down at the table and said, "I'm going to die." I started to cry, shaking my head, not wanting to hear what he was saying. He then said, "I'm proud of you, Lori. You'll make it just fine without me. Be tough!" Then I woke up. This was the only dream I've had of my father since his death.

I have always felt that I never completely accepted my father's death. My mother and brother always felt that I would fall apart when my father died because of the special relationship that I had with him. When I was called to the hospital, in the last few days of my father's life, my mother had a priest waiting for me just in case I

Never went to a funeral

Everybody leans on me

became too emotional. I was determined to show them that I was tough *I had to be strong for my mother.* and would not fall apart. Throughout the terrible time of my father's *she and my* death and funeral I was the tough one, the one that everyone leaned *father had 35* on. The terrible thing was that I was so busy being tough that I never *years* got the chance to realize that my daddy was gone. Suddenly, it hit me *together* that I had to learn to live without him.

I feel that the dream helped me to accept the fact that my father *and* is gone. Time will also help me to deal with my loss and learn to live *to deal* with it. Eventually, I feel that I will be able to think back on my *with the death of my* father and smile, for no one can take my memories away. The dream also *brother* made me realize that, just as I did as a little girl with my drawings, *seven days later* I am still looking for my father's approval. Somehow, through this dream I feel that I have received it.

II. REHEARSING

In Chapter Two you saw and tried several different rehearsal strategies for beginning a paper. For this activity, use the one that seems most comfortable to you. Many students prefer to begin a writing assignment with freewriting, just as Steve Shaver did for "Hidden Bitterness."

Remember, freewriting is a "trial run," a way for you to see what your ideas and impressions might be and a way of recording everything that's on your mind about what you have just read. Here you are writing simply as a way of finding your way to a topic or tentative topic, or of seeing the direction your ideas or experiences are taking.

Now freely write about a number of ideas or associations you made with the assigned reading including your thoughts and feelings about them. Since you are only testing possibilities here, try out as many as you can.

At this stage, write quickly, postponing concerns about correct grammar, spelling, punctuation, or organization. Think of this rehearsal as an opportunity for free, uncensored, exploratory writing.

COLLABORATING

Once you have completed writing down your ideas or associations, exchange papers with one or more of your classmates. As you look over your partner's writing, think about what topics seem appealing to you. What would you like to hear more about? Which topic or topics seem most interesting? Are there a couple of ideas that you think the writer might like to explore or would benefit from pursuing? Discuss your selections with him, giving the reasons for your choices.

If your partner chose to write about one association only and used this rehearsal as a way of considering what he or she wants to say and possibly how to organize it, what is your reaction to it? Do you think it is a good idea? Is it worth pursuing? Should your partner stick with it or try something else?

After your partner or others in your group have read your writing and selected an idea or two that seem appealing, see whether their selections are ones that you would like to develop further. You, of course, may decide that you prefer another idea, one that seems more compelling to you as a writer. If so, let your instincts be your guide.

COLLABORATING

With the members of your group or with the entire class, consider some of the topics you have just seen.

What were a couple that interested you, that you would like to hear more about? Was anyone discouraged from pursuing a particular topic? Why?

Is there a relationship, do you think, between the topic you choose and the success of the paper you develop from it? If so, what is it?

What might make a good topic from a reader's point of view?

What is a good topic, do you suppose, from the writer's point of view?

In what specific ways, do you think, the two points of view—the reader's and the writer's—might be the same?

As a way of summing up, how would you now define a "good" topic?

As a way of summing up, how would you now define a "good" topic?

COLLABORATING

Take one or more of your chosen topics, which may be either a single idea or an experience you want to relate, and *talk it through* with a partner or the members of your group. Take a few minutes, sit back, and tell as much as you can about the idea or incident you want to relate or describe. Take turns telling and listening.

For this stage you will freely write as much as you can about the idea or experience you just talked through with your partner. Because a reader is interested in the same kinds of information that a listener finds interesting, try to include the same kinds of details that you told your partners. Your aim here is to include as much as possible. Still think of this as a trial run, a rehearsal, where you can try out ideas, add information, and concentrate on quantity, knowing that you can later omit material since at this stage you are still essentially writing for yourself.

If you already have a fairly well developed idea from your freewriting, talking it through may have reminded you of other details or information you can now add. At this stage, you are still exploring your topic to determine if it is worth pursuing or if you have enough information to make it work for you.

Or in the course of writing have you discovered another topic? If so, try it out. When writing is seen as a process, it often leads in unexpected directions. In fact, much of the satisfaction of writing comes from this act of discovery.

At any rate, the objective here is to produce enough raw material to begin drafting.

III. DRAFTING

In spoken conversation a listener can question or help fill in details of what you are trying to say. In writing, however, the reader has only your paper from which to understand what you are saying. This means that at some point in the writing you have to take the perspective of the reader—becoming the reader when you write. There may be a difference between what you want to write and what you have actually recorded on paper.

The prize-winning papers clearly demonstrate that the writers wrote with readers in mind, and though certainly not exactly alike, the essays share many of the same characteristics.

Focus

Each of the essays shows that the writer is fully aware of the potential confusion that would result for a reader who meets a series of shifting or unrelated ideas. Thus, the essays are highly controlled; that is, each one is focused, or unified, around one central idea or incident. The writer does not get sidetracked or drift from the focus by including anything unrelated or irrelevant but sticks to the dominant topic. This is clear in the brief piece by Sharon Myers about the end of a relationship, and in Tom Dyser's essay about his accident.

This is also true for Setsuko's "Open Ocean," p. 110, which may appear to be less focused than the others because it is broken into parts. But these are actually a series of events which relate to each other because they are focused around a specific time in her life.

Development

A second characteristic is that each essay not only is focused but is fully developed through supporting information. Depending on the intention, the writer does this by *describing* an incident, person, or place, *narrating* or relating an experience, or *explaining or analyzing* a feeling or idea. In most cases, however, the writer chooses as the supporting information a combination of these.

Whatever method of development the writer chooses, he or she also includes the *significance* of what is being described, narrated or explained. She either states the significance directly or strongly implies it so that the reader understands or senses *why* the event or idea was meaningful.

For instance Sharon Myers' piece is a narrative; that is, it relates an experience between her and the man in her life. What makes her essay so powerful is that it also strongly implies the significance or the importance that the event had on her, although it is not directly stated. Unlike Sharon Myers, David Reed, in his narrative (p. 124), directly explains what the incident about him and his father means to him. He does this in the very first sentence: "While visiting my father recently, I suddenly realized how the years have brought about a reversal of roles in our relationship."

In the final two sentences of her description, Lu Ann Deveny also directly states the significance of the view before her: "I feel as if this window was placed in my little laundry room for my own sole purposes of strength and enjoyment. This is not just a window; it is a gallery filled with my private thoughts, feelings, and treasures." Joe Adams' description, on the other hand, strongly implies the impact that watching the dying chicken had on him so that the reader senses why it was meaningful.

Regardless of the manner in which it is done—whether you narrate, describe, or explain—the purpose of the supporting information is to recreate in the mind of the reader the experience you are writing about so that he or she can see what you saw, feel what you felt, and think what you thought—and understand why it mattered. What was subjective and personal now becomes public and understandable to someone other than the writer.

The only essays that do not include significance as a necessary ingredient are the final two essays in Chapter Four, Daniel Luther's "Pre-Realization" and Janine Blank's "Learning from Apes." In these, the writers strived to appear objective, more scientific, excluding their personal imprints and their feelings about what they were writing.

Structure

Another characteristic of each essay is its sense of structure. That is, information is arranged so that it is easy for a reader to follow. Brent Jones, for example, in "My War With Stress" (p. 100) discussed a number of stress-related experiences in the order in which they occurred, beginning with being drafted and his duty in Vietnam, his subsequent reenlistment and marriage, and finally his police work and marital difficulties. His narration not only supports his point, but the chronological or time order makes it easy to follow:

> "October 26, 1970, . . . I was drafted . . . .
>
> When I arrived in Viet Nam, . . .
>
> Then two months before I came home, . . .
>
> Then finally the day came to go home . . . It was nine in the morning
>
> October 25, 1972 . . . .

During the first year following my discharge, . . . I ended up reenlisting . . . .

I met my wife and we were married two months before my second discharge . . . .

I became a police officer . . . .

. . . she couldn't handle the stress anymore, so she called it quits to our marriage . . . .

In January, 1986, . . . "

The reader can also easily follow Lue Ann Deveny's description of the changing world outside her window (p. 130) because it is arranged in a seasonal sequence:

"Outside the window, the changing seasons each create their own unique painting . . . .

Spring brings an exciting view of wet, black bark . . . .

Summer's portrait is peaceful and quiet . . . .

I think fall is my favorite season . . . .

At last my sleepy winter portrait has arrived . . . . "

Kevin Larcher, in paragraph two of his essay "My Summer Job", (p. 140) moves spatially from top to bottom in his description of the mountain area around Lake Tahoe. This makes it easy for the reader to picture:

"Encircling my view, the mighty Sierra Nevada Mountains stood proudly . . .

Tall evergreens blanketed the feet of these rocky, snow-capped mountains . . .

Down below, surrounding the lake, a shoreline of massive granite boulders

. . . Along the shore . . . . "

Mike Greene's description of the cocktail lounge in "Don't Shoot the Piano Player" (p. 137) is structured so that the reader moves naturally with Mike from the parking lot and the outside of Dee's 41 Club to the inside of the lounge with its customers, padded bar, juke box, and piano:

Dee's 41 Club was nestled between an adult bookstore and an auto supply outlet . . . Even the graffiti on the peeling exterior was dated . . . .

We parked the car and walked inside . . . Directly in front of us and extending to the left was the bar . . . .

I learned over the torn padding on the bar and asked the bartender for change for the jukebox . . . .

I walked over and sat down on two milk crates that were being used for a piano stool . . . . "

Personal Voice

Another similarity among many of the essays is that the writing is personalized. The reader can often sense the personalities of the writers in it. This quality helps establish a relationship between the writer and the reader, connecting one human being with another. It is also what makes the reader want to read. It is sometimes referred to as authenticity, or honesty, or personal voice, even commitment, and it makes the writing seem to be more than just an academic exercise.

Correctness

And, finally, an obvious characteristic of the essays is that they all have been carefully proofread to eliminate errors that distract from a reader's enjoyment. Serious mistakes in writing can actually confuse the meaning of what is being said, and are especially annoying because they put the burden of understanding on the reader.

COLLABORATING

As you think about shaping your writing for a reader, you might look at Steve Shaver's final version of "Hidden Bitterness" (p. 128) and consider with your classmates the following questions:

1. Does the piece focus on one dominant thing? If so, what is it?

2. In what specific ways does Steve develop "Hidden Bitterness"?
    Does he describe an incident, person, or place?
    Does he narrate or relate an experience?
    Does he explain or analyze a feeling or idea?
    Does he include the significance of the event? If so, is it directly stated or implied?

3. What about the piece made it easy to follow?

4. What does the writing say about the writer?
    Does he care about his subject?
    Does he sound committed?
    What about the writing makes it seem real?
    What do you think he might be like as a person?

 In the last writing assignment on p. 69, you talked through with your partner one (or more) of your ideas as preparation for writing. You then freely wrote about the idea or experience. This material now needs to be shaped for a reader by putting it in draft form.

COLLABORATING

Since you are no longer just writing for yourself but for a reader, it is a good idea to get a reader's opinion. For this activity, exchange the drafts you just completed with one or more classmates.

Your aim is to get feedback from readers other than yourself—your classmates, your instructor—so that you can eventually become more objective in viewing your own writing from a reader's standpoint. This will enable you eventually to become your own reader as you write.

Consider the following questions *before* you read each other's papers.

What do you like about the paper? What did the writer do well? Be as specific as you can about this.

In what ways as outlined below can the writer improve the paper?

1. Does the piece focus on one dominant thing?
   If so, what is it?
   Is everything else related to it?
   Is this a "good" topic; that is, is it one that someone other than the writer would find thought provoking or worth pursuing?
   Or does the paper suggest a different topic that would be worth pursuing in another draft?

2. Since the writer's purpose is to help the reader see what he saw, feel what he felt, and think what he thought, to make the writing fully understandable, think about the following:
   Are you uncertain about anything in the piece?
   Is there information in segments or sentences that is confusing or incomplete?
   Might the writing be improved and made more satisfying for you as a reader if there were more details?
   Could there be more explanation to help your understanding?
   Is there enough information to make the paper work?
   Is the *significance* either directly stated or implied?
   What other suggestions do you have to help the writer develop his point?

What other suggestions do you have to help the writer develop his point?

3. Does it have a sense of structure?
   Is the information arranged so that it is easy for a reader to follow?
   Is there something that seems out of order?
   If so, why?

4. Does it seem that the writer cares about the subject?
   How can you tell that from the writing?
   What about the writing makes it seem real?
   Can you sense the personality of the writer in it?
   Can you point to any passages, even individual words or phrases, where the writer's personal voice comes through?
   On the other hand, does this quality seem to be missing?
   Why? Where specifically?
   Does it sound as though the writer is merely fulfilling an assignment?
   What makes you think so?

First read your classmate's paper once to yourself to get an overall feel for it.

Then read it to yourself a second time, noting its strengths; using the questions above, also note in what specific ways it might be improved for you as a reader. It is helpful to jot down some notes on a separate piece of paper.

To let the writer hear his paper being read aloud, you might now read his paper to him. By hearing it read aloud he may note the difference between what he wanted to write and what he actually recorded. He may also become aware of some things he wants to change.

Discuss with the writer what you have noted about his paper, both strengths and weaknesses.

Actually, it is very unlikely that any writer's first draft is so satisfying to him or his reader that it does not need some rethinking and rewriting. Only you can decide the direction of your writing, however. Even if you and your readers are generally satisfied with your initial draft, most likely it still needs some minor work, such as clearing up any uncertainties, providing additional information, eliminating unnecessary words or phrases, probably even some rearranging so that the piece reads more smoothly or logically.

In fact, many writers make major changes from draft to draft. They may even change topics altogether or attempt to come at the topic from a different direction or perspective. Or perhaps they have good ideas they want to write about but are dissatisfied with the ways in which they have developed them. You will recall the changes Steve made from draft to draft in his piece, "Hidden Bitterness." Also, you may have noticed that as late as Draft 3, when "the pieces finally started to come together," Steve fell back on freely writing as a rehearsal for what would become his final draft.

This process of freewriting, drafting, collaborating, and redrafting is a cycle that you may need to go through more than once. Some writers will be so attracted to certain topics that right from the start they may have a good idea of the direction their paper will take and so will need fewer trial runs. This might be the case for you. For others, the process of writing will take them from one idea to the next because they will use the writing process to think about the topic.

Revise your draft or write as many drafts as necessary given the feedback and your intentions.

In practice, this may mean having your paper read or reading it yourself *several times* to different members of your own group and even members of other groups or your instructor. Each time your paper is read, take notes on the feedback you get to help you redraft.

This collaborative technique will be helpful whenever you write a paper.

ACTIVITY

The following papers, written by several basic writing students, will give you practice in objective evaluation, looking for both strengths and weaknesses in a piece of writing in relation to the criteria of *focus*, *development*, *significance*, *structure*, and *personal voice*. Whether done in groups or with the entire class, it also will be useful practice for your own drafting and revising.

Several readers' responses, which follow the first paper about Brownie the hamster, are included as an example to get you started.

A.

One sunshiny day Brownie, our hamster, got sick with a tumor
right above his testicles. I grew very upset about this, so Mike and I
took him to the veterinarian, and the only possible way he could say it
was a tumor or cancer was to open him up and remove his testicles. Mike
and I agreed and we would know by Monday at the latest. Sunday the vet
called and told me that Brownie didn't survive the surgery, so we
could pick him up or have Brownie destroyed. I chose to take Brownie
home to be buried. I didn't know how on earth I was going to tell Mike
because this was his pet, and I wasn't going to be home to comfort him
in any way possible. I called Mike and told him that Brownie didn't
make it. Mike asked ''Why didn't he make it? How come he couldn't live
any longer? What did the vet say? When can we pick him up?'' I had only a
few answers to these questions. Finally, Monday came, and it seemed
like it dragged on forever until 4:15, time to go to the vet. We left
for the vet, and he asked us to come back to the laboratory. He put his
hand into a cardboard box. My heart was in my stomach about to be sick.
Mike was so choked up that he couldn't tell the vet he didn't want to
see Brownie. Now all this time since Sunday we had thought he was dead.
But to our surprise, the vet pulled out Brownie, who was alive running
on the table. I was so overwhelmed with joy that I was crying. We took
Brownie, who had seven bite-size stitches on his bottom, home. We had
to give him penicillin which he kept spitting up all over his fur. Mike
had to put ointment on Brownie's eyes so they wouldn't stay shut
forever. Nobody thought or believed that he had made it. The vet said

he would like to see him in ten days to take the stitches out. He was very optimistic. The ten days came and went by so fast we were back at the vet's. Mike went into the laboratory, and I stayed out in the waiting room. Mike kept making weird faces each time the vet yanked stitches out, and Brownie squealed so loud that I could hear it in the waiting room. Finally the vet was all done, and we were on our way home with Brownie who looked like he ran a marathon. Brownie lived quite well for the next three months. Consequently, I was surprised. When Mike called me at 6:30 one morning, he was so upset that he couldn't find the words to tell me that Brownie lost his life. I was stunned; part of me wanted to go to Mike's and really see if it was true; the other half wanted to stay in bed. After church Mike and I went to his house to bury Brownie. I had to pick Brownie up and put him in a plastic bag. Brownie was stiff as a board and so cold that he was very disgusting to pick up. Eventually we both buried him in Mike's backyard. From that miraculous day that he came back to life, I still can't believe he lived that long with all the trauma in his tiny body.

"Great opener—sure caught my attention"

"I like the way the writer included her reactions and feelings."

"The part about Brownie squealing was good. I could almost hear him."

"From the first sentence, I wanted to keep reading it. I didn't have any problems following what she was saying."

"What a crazy story, but I know it's true because you couldn't care that much about something you made up and the details made it seem so real."

"I liked the story, but who is Mike?"

"I got confused about why you thought Brownie was dead. I got a little mixed up there."

"I didn't get the part about the ointment and his eyes staying shut forever."

"That one sentence towards the end, 'Consequently, I was surprised' confused me. Do you mean that you were surprised that Brownie lived quite well or that he died? Maybe you need to rearrange that part a little bit so it will be clearer."

B.

Reading Lorraine Fogg's ''Staying Tough,'' in which she was always searching for her father's approval, reminded me of my own search for my mother's love. Being the only girl with two brothers, my feelings were affected the most. For example, when my mom was there, we could have girl-to-girl talks, but I just couldn't talk to men about that. My mom and I were so close that we would go shopping together, and I would help around the house. Throughout my entire life my mom's love was really important to me. Six years ago my parents got a divorce. Any divorce is traumatic, but my parents' divorce was devastating. My mother did not want custody of us. I love my father very much, but the idea that my mother didn't want me was very painful. Many things have happened in those six years without my mom that I would have loved to share. For instance, I would have loved to have her help with prom, see me on graduation day receiving my diploma, and have her be there on my birthday. Even though I'm an adult, I still miss my mom's love. Last year was the first time I saw her since the divorce. I laid eyes on her, and I wanted to speak, but nothing came out because I was nervous. It was a very confusing reunion. On one hand, I was thrilled to see her, and the rest of me was furious for leaving me behind. The visit was very difficult for both of us. She attempted to explain the complicated reasons why she had left and not taken me with her. Her personal confusion started when she was looking for her real mother. By this time, she found out she was adopted at the age of two. At the age of thirty-six she found her real mother. This real mother changed my mom's life dramatically. My mother became very active as an Evangelist. This religion condemned our way of living. For example, my father drank an occasional beer. According to her religion this was forbidden. My brothers and I, being normal teenagers, listened to rock music, and she told us we were worshipping the devil. The visit ended on a very sour note. My mother disapproved of my way of life, and I felt confused, rejected, and unloved. My feelings about my mother affected my whole life. I had a constant upset stomach, and I would cry myself to sleep. Finally, after three months of this constant upset, my friend Heidi said we should talk. I didn't want to talk to her because she had both her parents, and how could she understand how I felt, but she kept at it, and eventually, I opened up to her. The one thing she said to me changed my outlook toward my mom. She said, "You've got to grow up and accept the way your mom is, no matter what. She loves you and she will always be your mom. You have to accept her love the way she gives it!" After that talk I really started looking and taking things differently. I spent less time wishing that she was the way I wanted her to be. I still miss her, and I wish she was around. I have reached the point where I know I still have my mom's love.

C.

In "At Last, Relief," Tom Dyser's shock and disorientation at suddenly realizing his hands had been crushed by a powerful clamp while he was working reminded me of an accident I had at the age of six that left me confused and emotionally distraught. At the time of the accident, I was so involved in playing and arguing with my little brother, Ray, that I could hardly believe the accident actually happened. My brother and I kept our crayons in a five-pound coffee can, and as usual, we were arguing over who gets to use what color crayon first. Searching for that particular crayon, I leaned over the coffee can to look inside, and before I realized what happened, Roy had thrust my head down into the sharp edges of the can. Feeling no pain and seeing no blood, I looked up at my brother and saw a wave of shock come over him. Bursting into tears, he shrieked for our mother. Confused, I wondered why he was hollering for our mother because it wasnt' like him to call for our mother whenever he did something nasty to me. I reasoned that because I didn't feel any pain I was all right. I still didn't understand what had happened as my mother ran toward me hysterically chanting, "Oh my God, oh my God." She swooped me up off the floor and laid me down on the couch, and as she raced toward the telephone she sternly ordered me to stay there and keep my head back. It was then that I realized something was wrong with me, that I must be hurt and it must be bad enough to cause my brother and my mother to be upset. Frightfully bewildered by the reaction my brother and mother were having, I wanted to look at the injury to see for myself just how scary it looked. The next thing I remember is how angry and repulsed my father was when he walked into the front room and saw me on the couch. He began to hotly swear at my mother, "Goddamit Mary, why can't you keep there kids under control? Now just look at Denise. Jesus Christ!" And as he glanced my way he gravely shook his head in disgust. My imagination began to create all sorts of terrible visions of how bad I looked. I wondered if my nose fell off or something. Dumbfounded, I thought it still wasn't possible for me to really be hurt bad because of the lack of pain. I had to find out what was going on, but I was reluctant to ask my parents because they were already upset with me, and I didn't want to get into any more trouble. My parents marched me upstairs and put me to bed, insisting that I stay there, or else. But, just as soon as they left the room, I bounced out of bed and bravely looked at my startled reflection in the mirror. I was abruptly shocked to see a red, gaping, bloodless gash about a half-inch deep, and an inch wide on the bridge of my nose, between my eyes. Panicking, and confused by the lack of pain and blood, I thought I looked deformed, mutilated, and gross. I imagined how awful I would look in stitches, like a Frankinstein monster, and when the neighborhood kids see me that way they will turn away from me in terror. I wondered if this freak accident happened to me because I had been a bad girl. Remembering the way my parents reacted when they saw me, their disgusted expressions and harsh tones of voice made me wonder if they no longer loved me because I was so ugly. I became very distraught over the idea that I might never look normal again. Magnifying my fears, I wanted to hide my face forever so that I wouldn't scare anybody else, so I dejectedly crawled back into bed and pulled the covers way up over my head. The accident must have drained me emotionally because I immediately fell into a deep sleep.

D.

While reading the devastating article "At Last Relief," a horrifying incident Tom Dyser relived of having his hands sandwiched between a ton of metal, my own memories of pain endured when the tip of my middle fingers was smashed was vividly brought back. I was visiting my best friend Diane at her parents' hundred acre farm in southern Ohio. One afternoon, for a little fun in the sun, Diane and I mosied about a half mile down their property to a crystal clear, ice cold, fresh running water creek. Deciding to be creative, we attempted to build a dam out of gigantic rocks that lay on the bottom of the creek, up and down its bank, and all over the ground. I, having just ever so carefully placed a rock down, was taken by total surprise when a monstrous boulder came crashing down on top of my fingers. Letting out a scream that could curl the hair on a pig's back, petrified from top to bottom, I stood with my eyes glared to the piece of pale white finger that dangled by a thread of skin. Overcome by chills of horror and disbelief, my legs softened to rubber, my head spun, and my stomach turned inside out. Dazed and confused, I held my finger tightly and ran away leaving Diane in a state of shock.

Treading through fields of cow manure, running up steep hills, and jumping over a barb-wired fence, I felt like I weighed a ton and was moving in slow motion. Only one thing ran through my mind, like getting to the hospital yesterday! Up to this point I was numb and hadn't really felt the pain, but now it was getting the best of me. My finger was burning like a raging fire out of control, pulsating as fast as a bunny's heart, and felt like it was being pressed through a meat grinder. There was no bleeding, thank goodness, but it looked equally gross and disgusting. Still running to the house, I was having delusions of being at the hospital already, having my finger saved and freed from the excruciating pain. In the car, on the way there, I did my best to keep calm, but I know I was squirming up and down in the seat, making uncontrollable noises from the pain. After getting to the hospital, there was no immediate relief given to me. Feeling as though someone was repeatedly stabbing and tearing at my entire arm to my finger, I lay waiting for about an hour for the doctor. Much to my dismay, no freedom of pain came for months due to the nerves being exposed, and anything barely touched it sent sharp, penetrating tinges through my finger clear up to my teeth. It was unreal! After several months of out-patient care, the pain eased; however, my finger never quite looked, felt, or worked the same.

E.

Reading of the emotional distress Tom Dyser experienced and wrote about in his article, "At Last Relief," reminded me of an emotionally traumatic experience in my own life. I was ten years old and was in Children's Hospital to have my tonsils and adenoids removed. I was admitted to the hospital the night before the operation and had spent a sleepless night worrying about what would happen to me at seven-thirty the next morning when my surgery was scheduled. At around seven o'clock in the morning, I climbed onto a cart and was taken from my room down to the surgical floor and left unattended in the corridor outside the operating room. Thus abandoned, my worries began to intensify slowly into terror. I would see doctors and nurses clad in green surgical garb going about their business, which seemed to include ignoring an extremely anxious boy in plain sight of them. On one of the walls hung a large clock, and I could clearly see its hands slowly move toward the time of my appointment with whatever horrible fate awaited me. No one had told me exactly what would happen; consequently, I didn't know what to expect. Whatever was going to happen, I was terrified of it. As that big hand crept toward that big six, I grew so distraught I started to cry, but still no one consoled me. Seven-thirty passed; now I was in a state of panic. Finally I was wheeled into the operating room, where I was forced to climb onto a table directly under a painfully blinding light. I lay on my back surrounded by strangers who were covered from head to toe in green with only their eyes showing. They didn't look human; instead they looked like monsters from a horror movie, and I was their victim. My feeling of panic grew even worse. Someone strapped down my legs; now I couldn't escape. Someone else placed thick heavy gauze over my eyes; now I couldn't see, but I still felt that bright light. What were they going to do now? Suddenly, everything went black. My face felt a stinging sensation; then came that evil smell--that odor from hell! I couldn't breathe; I was being poisoned! Then came the voice of my torturer; it was my own pediatrician, the man who had told me I needed this operation; he had arranged to administer the anesthetic. He was telling me to breathe deeply and count backwards. I wouldn't cooperate with this villain; no way was I going to breathe this poison if I could help it. I wanted to do him physical harm, but I was strapped to a table, couldn't see, and was vastly outnumbered by those green creatures. The only parts of my body left free were my arms; they were wildly flailing about in a futile effort to both escape from my agonizing torture and attack that sadistic quack. Alas, the poison proved too much for me; against my will I inhaled the ether, and I slowly began to lose consciousness. I felt my very existence slowly sink downward until it seemed I had sunk below my body. For an instant the smell and burning disappeared; then I felt nothing.

F.

I read a passage today called ''Staying Tough.'' It was about a
girl and how she dealt with her father's death. One statement in there
which I can easily relate to is that her father could always see right
through her just like my dad can. No matter whenever I did something
wrong and I had to face my dad, he could usually see right through me.
It was almost as if he was psychic. The thing I would do most often is
tear up farm machinery, never once on purpose. Stuff just seemed to
happen, usually because I wasn't paying attention to what I was
doing. Dumb stuff just seemed to happen. I'd be sitting on the tractor
working ground. Then I would look back to check what was happening,
and for no reason something would be broken. Most of the time the
breaks were caused by general wear on the machinery and couldn't be
helped. Once in a while I would do something stupid. What usually got
me in trouble was I would pull out of the field and try to fix it myself
so dad wouldn't get mad when he came home from work. You don't know my
dad, but when he gets mad he goes wild, and I mean wild. There is
nothing in the world that would get him madder than when I tore up
machinery. Repairs were usually expensive and hard to fix, time
consuming, and of course they always happened at the worst possible
time. What usually got me in trouble was I would fix it and not fix it
right. Then it would just break again. When something breaks once,
it's bad enough, but when it breaks twice, it's usually irreparable
and costs a lot of money to fix. With me being the way I am, I only learn
the hard way. So we went through this process many times.

G.

I read Lorraine Fogg's story about ''Staying Tough,'' and I have
some similar things that happened to me that caused me to stay tough.

I remember when I was six or seven my grandfather was like my best friend. My grandparents had a farm of 110 acres. He would put me on his shoulders, and we would walk through the pastures, looking at the cows and horses. He would always cut me sugarcane off of a stalk that looks a lot like a corn stalk. I would eat and play until I was exhausted. He always called me Sampson, and he would say, "Hey Sampson, want to go for a ride?" I would reply "Yeh," and we would ride his pick-up truck through muddy water and down the truck path. I remember him singing his favorite song, and I would be there just smiling and he always said, "What are you smiling at?" I would say, "At you grandpa." He was some man. My dad was his youngest son, and I was my dad's oldest. I don't know why I was his favorite grandson, but I kind of liked the idea. As I got older I was always talking about going to see Papa and all of those animals they had. This one summer of 1974 we went back to Newport, Arkansas because we had heard that he was terminally ill and he wasn't looking too good. So everyone in the family was going to see our grandfather. When we got there, it didn't seem like the same place. Everyone was in the back room on the south side of the house. He didn't look like my grandfather, and I was kind of scared. Later I asked my mom, "Why does Papa look the way he does?" And she answered, "Your Papa is dying." My mother said he was very sick. I didn't ask any more questions pertaining to my grandfather. We stayed down there for another few days. Then we came back to Akron, Ohio. It wasn't three months later that he died. His death shook everyone, but I was numb; I didn't know how to act. I guess since I was the oldest grandson, I was trying to keep my composure in front of my brothers and sisters until the day of the funeral when they were putting him in the ground. I was hysterical, and my father came to

calm me down by saying, "He was my father too." My grandfather has

been dead for thirteen years now. And looking back through my

memories, I smile, and try humming his favorite song. At times I

wonder to myself if he was still alive if he would be proud of me for

the things I have done. Now that I'm much older I know the meaning of

"tough." Tough doesn't mean that you can't cry or weep. Tough means

being able to accept the fact that nature takes its course and hope

you are man or woman enough to realize it. Because I have finally

accepted my grandfather's death, I'm tough.

IV. EDITING

At this stage in the writing you have written what you intended to write, which may have involved a number of drafts, and have readied your writing for a reader. So now all concerns about content and form are behind you.

In the publishing business writers turn their final drafts over to what is called a copyeditor, whose job it is to make whatever *corrections* are needed before the manuscript is printed. The copyeditor does not change the content or meaning of a piece of writing or the general shape it is in. It is the copyeditor's job, however, to correct any major problems with sentences, grammar, spelling, and the like. What she or he does is bring everything in line with standard forms and conventions so that the published piece of writing is easy for readers to read. Any mistakes, no matter how small, may distract and sidetrack the reader. Even though this last step is time-consuming and appears less important, perhaps, than the other stages in the process of writing a paper, it nonetheless has to be done.

Most likely you do not have a copyeditor to *proofread* and correct your final draft, but you do have yourself and your group. Putting all your heads together, you will likely take care of the same kinds of problems a copyeditor would because although you may not have mastered all the areas shown here, each of you will contribute what you do know.

COPYEDITING CHECKLIST

Sentence Problems

_____ Are there any incomplete sentences (fragments)?

_____ Run-together sentences?

_____ Tangled, confusing, awkward sentences?

_____ Are there any short sentences that could be combined?

_____ Are there any sentences with repeated words or ideas that could be eliminated or combined?

Punctuation Problems

_____ Are any periods—or other marks that show the ends of sentences—missing?

_____ Are there any places where commas should be used but are not?

_____ Are there any places where quotation marks need to be used?

_____ Are apostrophes used where they should be, to show possession?

Word Problems

_____ Are there any nouns whose -s endings are omitted but should not be?

_____ Are there any verbs whose -s endings are omitted but should not be?

_____ Are there any verbs whose -ed endings are omitted but should not be?

_____ Are there any incorrect verb forms used, such as *seen* instead of *saw* or *done* instead of *did*?

_____ Are there any incorrect forms of pronouns used (*I* vs. *me, he* vs. *him, she* vs. *her, they* vs. *them*)?

_____ Are any words incorrectly capitalized?

_____ Are there any words not capitalized that should be?

_____ Are there any misspelled words?

_____ Are there any wrong forms of sound-alike words used (homonyms)?

_____ Any inappropriate or incorrect word choices?

COPYEDITING STRATEGIES

Two major strategies to use in order to successfully edit your paper are 1) reading your paper aloud, relying on your own intuition about language, and 2) using sources other than yourself, such as the members of your group, standard dictionaries, and grammar handbooks.

Sentence problems are easily heard by reading aloud. This technique, which takes time to develop, is an effective way to detect whether or not sentences sound complete, whether ends of sentences are punctuated correctly, and whether or not sentences sound tangled and confusing. You can also hear by reading aloud the awkwardness that results from a series of short sentences that contain a number of repeated words.

With incomplete sentences (sentence fragments) it is best to read aloud from the bottom up, beginning with the last sentence in the paper and working your way to the beginning of the paper, one sentence at a time. This technique allows you to listen more effectively to hear whether a sentence sounds complete or not because you are focusing on the sound of a sentence, which in most cases follows a regular sound pattern. You of course can hear if something is missing, such as in the group of words "When you leave this afternoon" or "If you don't believe me." These groups of words might sound complete in a conversation, perhaps as answers to questions, but when read aloud by themselves, you can hear that some information is missing.

When reading to find run-together sentences, that is, two sentences not separated with a period (or a comma and a coordinating conjunction such as *and* or *but*, or by a semicolon), it is helpful to read aloud, slowly, listening to where your voice drops slightly or where you pause. When this happens, stop and reread that group of words in order to determine whether or not it sounds like a whole sentence. If so, make two sentences by using a comma and a coordinating conjunction, or separate them with a period or a semicolon.

If you detect any sentence problems after reading your sentences aloud a number of times, you can rework the sentences until they sound better to you.

You might also use the reading aloud technique to hear whether or not *-s* and *-ed* endings are used where they should be, whether with verbs or nouns. This technique might also help determine whether you have used incorrect forms of pronouns. Other problems with words probably require that you consult an outside source such as a dictionary or handbook.

COLLABORATING

You might want to use the Copyediting Checklist as a guide when you proof-read and edit your final draft. It might be a good idea to attach a copy of the checklist to your final draft as it circulates to members of your group. They, in turn, will check off on the checklist any errors they see in your paper and indicate where in the paper corrections need to be made.

Once the errors have been pointed out, you then need to talk as a group to determine whether or not the feedback is accurate.

ACTIVITY

Whether done in groups or with the entire class, this activity will give you practice in editing your own papers. The first paper below, which has been altered, demonstrates how this is done. The second, which also has been altered, is for you to work on together.

I can relate to a story called "Staying Tough" which is about a girls father who died two years ago. That reminded me of my fathers death four years ago. I can still remember all the great times the family shared we were all very close. My father was a school teacher and a basketball coach. He was well known throughout the town and was missed by friends, family, and co-workers. My father died on a Tuesday after school. He stayed home from work that day to fix the car. When I came home little did I know what had waited when I arrived. I found my father passed out on the garage floor by the car. First I said, "What's up" and realized that the car was running and he was passed out. I checked his pulse, and there wasn't one and went inside the house to call the squad. He died two hours later of carbon monoxide posining. It was an accidental death. Carbon monoxide is a colorless odorless gas and can take your body in a matter of minutes especially in a small garage. I still remember that day, and will never forget it, but there are some nights I wonder if I will ever see him again. The death of my father had brought my brother, mother, and myself closer together through the tough times that we've shared together. I can still picture his face; furthermore, I will never forget the last few words he said to me.

COPYEDITING CHECKLIST

Sentence Problems

_____ Are there any incomplete sentences (fragments)?

__✔_ Run-together sentences?

_____ Tangled, confusing, awkward sentences?

_____ Are there any short sentences that could be combined?

__✔_ Are there any sentences with repeated words or ideas that could be eliminated or combined?

Punctuation Problems

__✔_ Are any periods—or other marks that show the ends of sentences—missing?

__✔_ Are there any places where commas should be used but are not?

_____ Are there any places where quotation marks need to be used?

_✔✔_ Are apostrophes used where they should be, to show possession?

Word Problems

_____ Are there any nouns whose -*s* endings are omitted but should not be?

_____ Are there any verbs whose -*s* endings are omitted but should not be?

_____ Are there any verbs whose -*ed* endings are omitted but should not be?

_____ Are there any incorrect verb forms used, such as *seen* instead of *saw* or *done* instead of *did*?

_____ Are there any incorrect forms of pronouns used (*I* vs. *me*, *he* vs. *him*, *she* vs. *her*, *they* vs. *them*)?

_____ Are any words incorrectly capitalized?

_____ Are there any words not capitalized that should be?

__✔_ Are there any misspelled words?

_____ Are there any wrong forms of sound-alike words used (homonyms)?

_____ Any inappropriate or incorrect word choices?

"Staying Tough" is a title to a paper I read about a girl who's father died and she had to stay tough for her family members to lean on. This title caught my attention because it relates to the sport of wrestling, in which I had to stay tough and hold my own ground. In wrestling the phrase "staying tough" means exactly what it says. Wrestling is a sport in which I try to put as much pain on my opponent as I can to make him turn or do what I want him to do. Alot of the pain that is put onto a wrestler is what most people would call cheating because if the referee saw it he would probably stop the match, but the ref misses alot. I have had opponents dig their nails into me, scratch me, elbow me, punch me, or whatever they can do to me that the ref does not see. For me to do a wrestling move on my opponent takes preperation. First there are three positions in wrestling, first position is neutral, which is when both wrestlers are on their feet, the second position is top, which is when one wrestler is on top of the other wrestler, finally the third position is bottom, which is when one wrestler starts underneath his opponent. I was never very good on bottom, so I spent alot of time there, and considering most of the painful moves are done from the top position I had to stay as tough as possible. For example there is a move called the guillotine, which sounds painful by itself, in which the top position wrestler basically takes the lower part of his opponents body one way and his opponents head and neck the other way and stretches him until the opponent finally gives up because he is in so much agony. Preperation for the moves is pain, pain, pain. This is why staying tough is an attitude that is important to any wrestler especially me. I was

different than most wrestlers about this attitude in that for most
wrestlers staying tough is acting like nothing can hurt them. I, on
the other hand, and a few other wrestlers I watched, stayed tough in a
calm collective way. I admit I hate pain just like anyone else, and I
don't brag taking pain like alot of wrestlers because there will
always be someone bigger who will take anyone at their word.
Basically wrestling is a sport in which little restraint is put on the
wrestler inflicting the pain, I am not talking big time championship
wrestling either. However, we do have some rules to protect the
wrestlers such as the one called "potentially dangerous." This is
when the ref will stop the match because one wrestler has the
potential to seriously hurt his opponent. Do not misunderstand me
about trying to hurt my opponent I don't try to put him in a wheelchair
or anything like that. I simply try to make him move into a position I
want him in by using moves which hurt or pressure points. Pressure
points, and everyone has them, are points where I could push with my
nuckle, fist, or knee and send a few seconds of excruciating pain
through my opponent's body and make him move or jump into a position
which I can take advantage of. Inflicting pain could be accidental
too. If you have ever had the wind knocked out of you then you know how
painful and scary that can be. I am not trying to make it sound like
wrestlers are the toughest meanest guys around, I am just not telling
you any of the many times I have lain on the mat stairing at the ceiling
asking myself what in the world I am doing to myself. I must be crazy,
and believe me I done that alot. Wrestling is a sport which demands a
few commandments such as strength, confidence, and so I have
explained "STAYING TOUGH" is pretty important too.

Chapter 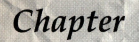 **4**

The Prize-winning Essays

The aim of this chapter is to provide through the prize-winning essays (1) a variety of writing topics to which you can respond using collaboration and the composing process presented in Chapter Three, (2) an opportunity for personally satisfying reading, and (3) models of successful writing by other developing writers like you.

As you recall from Chapter Three, you will write personal responses that associate your own ideas and experiences with those represented by the readings. These may take the form of identification with the writer, disagreement, or recognition of a shared problem. They may also help clarify your own understanding.

The twenty-two winning entries are arranged thematically ("Intense Personal Experiences," "Relationships: People," "Relationships: Places and Things," "Unexpected Outcomes," "Discovery") and include the student writers' commentaries.

INTENSE PERSONAL EXPERIENCES

SHARON MYERS
Cameron University (Oklahoma)
Roma Chenoweth, Instructor

We sat across the table, so close, but yet never farther apart. Seventeen years of our lives are spread out in neat little stacks between us. He wants his freedom, he says, no responsibilities, no one to answer to or look out for. I try to accept his reasoning. After all, he has always worked so hard providing for us and I know he loves me. So many things these days could account for his attitude, his just turning fifty, his job falling apart. Perhaps retirement and a little freedom are just what he needs to put the spring in his walk and the light back into his eyes. Everything is settled so calmly and he gets on a plane to go back to Nevada. Nine days later, at 2:45 a.m., I decide to give him a call, tell him I love him and see how things are going. A strange voice, definitely not belonging to the maid, answers the phone. Please, God, how do I put the light back in my eyes?

Sharon's Comments

We were asked to write a paragraph describing a personal experience. That day was my husband's birthday and I hadn't seen him in eleven months. I had spent all week trying to straighten out some real estate he had left tangled for me to handle. My biggest problem seemed to be finding a way to begin. After that, finding a place to stop and still make sense was extremely difficult. Being able to put some of my thoughts on paper really seemed to be a great relief.

BRENT L. W. JONES
University of Northern Colorado
Phillis S. Endicott, Instructor

My War with Stress

In discussing my problem dealing with stress, I feel that I must start at the very beginning with the role that the military played in my life. October 26, 1970, was a milestone because that was the day I was drafted by the United States Army. Having just graduated from high school and being nineteen years old made me a prime candidate for military indoctrination and training. Basic training during the early seventies consisted of a structured and a very disciplined environment where we recruits did what we were told, when we were told to do it. The training also taught us how to handle stress the military way, which meant that while under combat stress we had to do the job without regard for our own or other human lives. But it also taught us that basic human survival was essential. This lesson I learned very well; even fourteen years after Viet Nam, I am still trying to survive.

When I arrived in Viet Nam, my view of what the world was about was shattered. There I saw people living in grass huts and people starving. All the preconceptions that I grew up with, where everyone had a nice home and plenty to eat, were destroyed. In all my wisdom I never dreamed that people could live in poverty like the Vietnamese did. My first experience with the Vietnamese people came in Cam Rahn Bay. The second day I was there, I was placed on trash and garbage removal detail. Our job was to go around the replacement company and collect all the trash and garbage, load it onto a truck, and take it to the dump. At the dump all we had to do was let the Vietnamese unload the truck. When we arrived at the dump, we were met by a mob of hungry people who were supposed to unload the truck. The unloading started out in an orderly manner, but later, the people became an angry mob, grabbing for anything that was edible. We finally had to put a stop to this senseless violence because we were afraid for our lives, so we fired over their heads with an M–60 machine gun to disperse the crowd. We ended up unloading the truck for the rest of the afternoon. When we returned to the base, all of us were visibly shaken from the experience since it was only our second day in the country and our first combat experience in a war torn nation.

The next time stress came into play during my Viet Nam experience was the second week after I had arrived in the country. I was sent up north about twenty miles from the demilitarized zone on a fire support base called T-Hawk. By that time, I was assigned to the Second of the Five-O-First Infantry Battalion, One Hundred and First Airborne Division, for in-country training, because I was not trained in infantry tactics. During this period of training, we were only allowed three hours of sleep a night while we pulled perimeter guard. This assignment was designed to test how the new troops could handle the stress of combat. After three days of no sleep and not knowing if we would be alive in the morning or not, the pressure became too much for one of the men to handle, and he flipped out. The major problem we had was that he was in control of an M–60 machine gun. We finally got him stopped after he ran out of ammunition. Lucky for us, nobody was hurt, except that he had killed twenty head of water buffalo that were grazing in front of the bunker line.

The next night we were assigned to pull perimeter guard again. Everything was going fine until about one o'clock in the morning, when I noticed that there was a dead silence in the jungle—no bird or animal noises. I then heard what sounded like a jet flying overhead, but suddenly the jet engine stopped. The next thing I heard was someone yelling "Incoming!" From where I was, I turned around and saw the biggest explosion I have ever seen. This first 122-millimeter rocket hit our ammunition dump and there was shrapnel flying everywhere. For about the next two hours, the rockets kept exploding on the fire base. When the rockets finally stopped, we had about twenty minutes, which seemed like hours, before the North Vietnamese Army attack started.

That night I was in the guard tower about twenty feet from the wire. As I was looking out across the bunker line through the starlight scope, I saw the enemy troops approaching. I then got on the radio and called the 81-millimeter Mortar Platoon and directed them to fire illumination and high explosive rounds and to have the rounds fall about one kilometer in front of the bunker line. By then, all of the men in the fire base were out on the bunker line getting ready for the attack. When our first mortar round hit, it was like opening Pandora's Box; the enemy had started rushing the wire, screaming and yelling as they ran toward us. We then waited for the enemy to get closer before we opened up with our weapons.

When we finally received the order to fire, the whole bunker line lit up as bright as daylight; red and green tracers were flying everywhere. Explosion after explosion went off until one of the enemy's mortar rounds hit the tower where I was. After that, I don't remember much of what happened. All I remember is waking up in the unit hospital back in Cam Rahn Bay about two weeks later. To this day, I do not remember what happened after the mortar hit the tower. All I know is what the citation read. Basically it stated that, being wounded myself, I had helped in the medical evacuation of my fellow wounded soldiers, without regard for my own life. For this I was awarded the Silver Star, The Vietnamese Cross of Gallantry with Palm, and the Purple Heart.

In the next few months I continued to learn what war was all about. I became a paid killer with no feeling for right or wrong. I just went out day after day, not knowing whether I would be coming back from the mission or not. After about four months, I began to enjoy the killing and the adrenaline high I got from knowing what to expect from the jungle. Sometimes I would find myself volunteering for crazy missions, such as being a door gunner on a chopper—anything to get back into the jungle and to get that addicting high.

After a while I became an emotional refrigerator, not feeling death or caring about anyone or anything anymore. I was an empty void with nothing inside of me. I remember when my best friend Rich was killed. All I could do was stare at his lifeless shell of a body. I felt nothing, no remorse or even a sense of a loss, just another body. In other words, I became an emotional zombie of an unpopular war.

Then two months before I came home, all the fear and paranoia returned. Was I going to be the last sucker to die in this Godforsaken place? I found myself watching every move I made and every move the other men in my squad made, watching my front and back to be sure that no one was trying to kill me. Even during the rocket and mortar attacks, I was the first one in the trenches.

Finally, the day came to go home. I remember I received the word from the captain while we were doing a search and destroy mission outside the provincial capital of Huie. It was nine in the morning October 25, 1972. I packed my gear and boarded a plane bound for Travis Air Force Base outside San Francisco, California. Little did I know that eight hours later I would be entering a different type of war—one which I am still fighting—one within myself that I probably will be fighting for the rest of my life.

During the first year following my discharge, I found myself feeling that life was boring and useless. I tried to go back to my old job but it wasn't the same; something was missing. The excitement and the adventure were gone, so I ended up reenlisting in the Army for three more years. In the next three years everything went well. I worked hard and made it to the rank of sergeant. In the last year of my second enlistment, I met my wife and we were married two months before my second discharge.

Before I was discharged I decided that I wanted to make a career out of the military. But the only way I would consider making it a career was to earn my commission as an Army officer, and that required going to school. I started at a junior college in Colorado Springs, Colorado. Then I transferred to the University of Colorado, also located in Colorado Springs. In the meantime, my wife was still in the military and she had received orders to transfer to Fort Ben Harrison in Indiana, so I followed. In Indiana I started school at Indiana University located in Bloomington, Indiana. But in all the time I spent in school, I was bored and did only what was necessary to pass.

I then became interested in another career—one that would give me the excitement and adrenalin high that my life was missing. I became a police officer for the city of Indianapolis. The only difference I could see between the army and the police was that instead of fighting in the jungle I was now fighting in the city streets. Even when I was called to an automobile accident where the driver was killed, it was just like seeing another dead body: I felt nothing. I even found myself volunteering to work in the roughest black district in the city. It was just like Nam. I worked for the city for three years and then moved back to Colorado.

Because of the stress of the police job, the day finally came when I realized what I was doing to myself and family. I had taken my four-year-old son David out with me to serve a court summons on a rancher set up in northern Colorado. When I arrived at his ranch and approached him to serve the summons, he became very violent and I, for the first time, became afraid, not for myself, but for David. That was the day I decided to hang up the gun forever and never touch one again. But in the meantime, the stress from my work had become part of my personality and life. It also had taken its toll on my wife and she couldn't handle the stress anymore, so she called it quits to our marriage.

After she and I had separated, I felt that I didn't want anything to do with people anymore, because all people do is hurt other people and I had been hurt enough. I then moved into an apartment all by myself and I found myself staying away from people and society as a whole. During the summer months I would go up in the mountains and stay for months at a time, camping and living off the land, but this too soon came to an end.

In January 1986, I had had my fill of loneliness and depression. I couldn't handle my life anymore. I was out of control. I then went to a doctor about my depression and he recommended a special program that was just for Viet Nam Combat Veterans like myself. There I met ninety other men that had done the same stupid things that I had done. One thing I did learn was that I was responsible for my environment and I was the only person that could change it. As to the future, I now know that I will always have a problem dealing with stress, but it is how I manage the stress that is important.

When I was first drafted, I never would have guessed how severely the stress of Viet Nam would affect my life. But one thing I now know is how deadly and destructive stress can be. Of all the fifty thousand men that died in Viet Nam, twice that many Viet Nam veterans have killed themselves by their own hands since the end of the war. And I do not want to be another fatal statistic of one of the deadliest conflicts in our country's history.

Brent's Comments

The first problem I came across in writing this paper was, what am I going to write about. Luckily for me, the instructor gave me the choice of five topics; one was how I deal with stress, a subject I knew very well. As I started the paper, I found that I did not know where or how to start. I then decided that I should start at the very beginning from the time I was drafted up to the present. The first paragraph was the most difficult to write because all it did was bring back old, painful memories that I just wanted to keep buried deep inside my mind. After I finally did get started, I found that the ideas just kept coming. Another problem I confronted was what to write or delete from the paper. This was a hard decision to make because many things happened in that year that I feel are just as important as what I have written about in this paper. For the final draft it was basically rewording the sentences and correcting the punctuation and spelling, but the content basically stayed the same.

One of the best rewards I received from writing this paper is that I now know that I can write. Throughout my early school years all my teachers told me that I was a lousy writer and speller and I would never change; they gave up on me as a student. This caused me to hate reading, writing and English as a school subject for many years. But now I feel that I have been given a second chance in my writing skills. As for this paper, I am not finished with it yet. I am going back through it and filling in all the blank spots that I feel are important, no matter how long the paper is. It's a story that I feel needs to be told.

TOM DYSER
The University of Akron (Ohio)
Robin Herring-Conway, Instructor

At Last, Relief

The clamp that Bob, my partner, and I were working with had always left me in awe of its tremendous size and clamping ability. It's nearly six feet tall, weighs a full ton, and when clamped, it applies approximately twelve hundred pounds of pressure, per square inch, on anything that happens to be in its jaws. We have, on occasion, inserted a bent, half-inch thick, solid steel bar into the clamp and watched the bar straighten out as though it were made of warm plastic. After such an occasion, I commented to Bob how horrible it would be if anyone would get their hands caught in there. Hands caught in that clamp would turn to powder instantly. A year later, much to my horror, I found out exactly what it would be like. On April 10, 1984, we were setting up Press No. 1208, at B. F. Goodrich, for operation. The upper platent of the press was being equipped with a heavy pad that keeps it from burning the rubber belt after curing begins. This pad had a piece of old scrap material spliced to it. It was being drawn through the press when the scrap material broke. In an attempt to prevent the pad from slipping out of the machine, I, at the north end of the machine, pressed my weight, with both hands, on top of the pad inside the opened clamp. Bob, the operator, was at the opposite end, and was unable to see me. He wasn't aware of my hands being in the clamp. Without warning, he pulled the button which caused the clamp to close, crushing all of my fingers. Having turned my head for just a fraction of a second to look at the wall clock, I felt a pressure so great that I exploded into a scream that came from the abyss of Hell and went straight to the third floor of the shop. My eyes were as large as oranges and my mouth opened beyond its limits. The noise of stepping on popcorn while running down the theater aisle, as a small boy, came bursting into my crazed head. Every bone God put into my fingers crumbled into powder. My gloves were no protection against the savageness of its bite. Being in that clamp, for only seconds, seemed like an eternity. I thought relief would come when they opened it up, but it wasn't to be. My fingers felt as though somebody was holding them in a deep fryer. With my mind whirling, my breathing increased giving the impression of having sprinted the last fifty meters of a mile run. My speech became incessant. I repeated the Lord's Prayer over, and over, and over again, and again and again, and again. As they were wheeling me to the elevator, my feet were moving so rapidly that they thought I was convulsing. Between the Lord's Prayer and my heavy breathing I managed to tell them to leave my feet alone, for it helped. It didn't stop the pain, but it was a distraction for me. Oh God, my hands were on fire! Relief would come only when I went to surgery. Then they would put me under. The ambulance ride was swift and my incessant talking was swifter. The attendant glanced at my flattened hands but turned away. It was his first night on the job. At the emergency room a host of doctors and nurses met me, each having a specific job to perform. One put tubes in my nostrils giving me oxygen as they carted me to a room flooded with bright lights. A kindly nurse wearing a bright red sweater asked me questions about my family hoping that it would help distract my attention from the pain. "Let's get his clothes off and get him ready, Dr. Reef is on his way." "Get his wedding ring off." "Tom, we're going to take some x-rays, OK?" "I can't get the ring off. It's imbedded in his finger." "Can I have something to bite on. Please give me something." The kindly red sweater reached over and gave me a wet washcloth. As soon as it touched my lips, I began to shred it to pieces. My wife, now beside me, was holding it in my mouth. When I looked into her eyes, I could see we were truly made one, for her pain seemed even greater than mine. The ring finally came off after cutting. Nothing was felt; to experience more pain was not possible. As Dr. Reef stepped to my side and pulled back the covers to look at the damage done, a rush of tears filled my eyes for the first time. For such a large man he had the kindest and most compassionate face I'd ever seen. He had a real puzzle to work with. There were more pieces than there could be counted. With a calm and gracious voice, he assured me that putting puzzles together was his speciality, and was very good at it. With that, my pain subsided as they put me under for surgery.

Tom's Comments

When the class was told to write a descriptive paragraph, my thoughts went immediately back to my industrial accident in 1984. Still fresh in my mind, I felt a need to tell what it had been like having my hands crushed in a clamp. This assignment afforded me that opportunity.

The biggest and most significant change made during the writing process was on the initial freewrite draft. I tried to give the reader a sense of urgency and despair, which I felt during my ordeal, but it seemed to lose its effect with too much quoted conversation. It literally stopped the flow of the paper at that point. I then revised it by taking out a large portion of the conversation and left that which I felt was needed to give the reader a sense of being there. I was pleased with the result, for it seemed to bring the reader into the situation. Other changes were made throughout the paper's development, but only those which would lend themselves to give a more precise description.

Having to go over the accident in such detail was my greatest problem, for it still remains vivid in my mind. Losing Dr. Reef, my surgeon, to cancer shortly after my last surgery only enhanced the difficulty. We had developed an unspoken respect for one another. He, for my high spirited Christian attitude, and I, for his great compassion and surgical expertise. Losing a respected friend was more traumatic than losing my fingers. Having my paper considered worthy for competition was my greatest reward, and for that I am most grateful.

TRIEU PHAN
Merced College, Westside Center (California)
Mary Ann Edminster, Instructor

Escape

I became more frightened with every step after I had left "the camp." After a while, I began running. I ran so fast that I couldn't recognize what direction I should follow. Stopping for a while to determine where I was, I was startled by the alarm bell from the "re-education camp" to alert others that a prisoner had just escaped. Now I had to run at full speed.

Like other soldiers and workers of the old government, I had been in jail for two years in South Viet-Nam. I knew that I wouldn't be released and I didn't want to die in jail, so I had to do something. I decided escaping from jail was now necessary.

Running about one hour, I was so tired that I couldn't stand up although the thought of freedom kept me going. I then crawled to the nearest bushes, then I hid in them. I thought about my family. I recalled the words of my friend before he died, "You have to escape before we are transferred to the North . . . because they never release us." The soldiers with a pack of dogs walked speed-ily across the field. Suddenly, one of the soldiers separated and went toward my hiding place since his dog had barked. The bark was nearer and nearer. I dared not even to breathe, my body sweated, my limbs trembled at the thought of the death of my friend last week, since he had tried to escape. I didn't know what to do—stay here or run? My last thought was of God. I prayed "Please let me die, don't let them arrest me," and then I became unconscious.

It was dark and cold. The sound of insects woke me, and I recovered. I couldn't believe that I still was there. What happened to me? Why didn't the dog find me? I couldn't explain it, but I thanked God. Then I stood up and felt stronger than I had ever felt before. I continued with my escape and the hope of freedom.

Trieu's Comments

I have been in the U.S. for nine months. I was born in North Viet-Nam. As the Com-munists came to North Viet-Nam, my family had to move to the South. At that time, I was still a baby. Like other children, I went to school and then, later, graduated from high school. In 1975, the Communists came to South Viet-Nam. Later, being graduated from the university, I worked in a high school. As time went on, gradually I felt that my knowledge became poor and I forgot many things that I had learned in school; I began to study English at home. I used to listen to the broadcasts from another country at midnight. It was, of course, not legal in my country, but I wanted to practice listening English and know the news in the world.

After the coming of the Communists, there were so many incredible, miserable things and events that happened in my country. The story of this soldier was one of these events. This is the story which has a beautiful end that all the prisoners in the "re-education" camp wish. But the miracle couldn't happen to everyone.

SETSUKO KUWAHARA
Lane Community College (Oregon)
Doris R. Burkland, Instructor

By Open Ocean

1. *By Open Ocean*

That summer I spent in the fishing village was always hot. Summer in Japan is hot and very humid, but only one summer in my life was so hot and quiet.

I stood at the open ocean where we kids were evacuated from Nagasaki, our hometown. It must have been August 16 or 17, 1945, and I was thirteen years old. I had been standing for a long time rather absent mindedly.

I did not think, but I gazed at thick clouds that were white like snow. I sensed the breaking waves and blowing wind; I followed clouds with my eyes or with my soul. I knew nobody was there and nothing was there. The only one between heaven and earth was myself.

I could not think, but I was asking the sky something from inside my heart. I could not say clearly what it was, but I needed the answer.

It was August 15, in the morning a policeman and the village officers visited every house and informed the people that the emperor will make an important announcement at noon today. Villagers must listen to it respectfully. Villagers gathered in some houses which had a radio and heard the emperor, yet nobody understood what he announced. By the next day they only knew that the war ended. Although the villagers believed that Japan had won.

Nobody was excited; we were just exhausted. We were simply glad that we could sleep, turn on a light, take off dark long sleeved blouses, pants, hoods, and no longer hear the siren.

Time stopped; it seemed the villagers became extinct and that nature got back its origin.

2. *Best Job*

The war was everywhere; in fact, our small fishing village was prepared for the enemy's landing. The Japanese marines, which were called "Kamikaza" (suicide squad), and the Army came to the village. The villagers and our parents never thought such a small village could be a front; however, no doubt the open ocean was the Pacific Ocean. Besides that land was flat and no forts from old time; on the other hand the village was easy for landing.

In the village there were only kids, old people, women, and some people who were mentally or physically diseased. So kids who should have been in elementary school worked rather than being in school.

Our grandmother woke us before 5:30 a.m. so that we could go to work. Only five years old Fu-chan couldn't work, but she came sometimes and watched us. My sister, Misa-chan, who was 11, my brother, Ma-kun, who was 9, and my 7 year old brother, Nori-kun, and 12 year old myself dragged nets with our grandmother and the villagers.

The open ocean had huge, huge waves. We all had learned to swim in Nagasaki, my hometown, but we were afraid to enter the sea. Also we were forbidden to go in.

There were a few dragnets at night. In the morning the villagers and children pulled the nets by the ropes shouting, "yoi to se - - yoi to se - -." It took nearly one and a half hours. At the end, the shouting grew faster, "yo i to, yoito, yoito." Now only the men and several women were up to their waists in the water. The children took a break, and we were together with Fu-chan. She picked up very, very beautiful colored tiny stones like her finger tips.

Finally, the dragnet came to the beach, and the fishes jumping in the nets looked bright.

Behind the windbreak of tall, old, pine trees, pots of boiling water were waiting for the white, tiny fish.

I could take fish home in my apron as pay, and I could earn some money for the first time. It was not an easy job, but I enjoyed it.

My daily job at home was to draw two full buckets of water from a well. I carried them on a pole that nearly reached the ground, and it took fifteen minutes to carry the water home. I carried water several times a day.

Another routine at home was to grind wheat into flour. I never wavered with my routine because my sister Misa-chan was weak. I thought I should do the work of Misa-chan's and mine; also, my small aunt hated to get the water since the military came.

Instead of going to school, we were assigned to a farmer's house. There we planted rice, cut barley-wheat, manured the field, and took manure from houses with a cow-pulled cart.

Compared with these, the dragnet was fun.

3. *A Fishing Village*

There was a low, narrow mountain range between the open ocean, which was the Pacific Ocean, and Urado Bay. The village was formed at the foot of the mountains by the edge of the sea. The area between the bay and the mountains was narrow, so in some places houses stood only on the hill side.

The village became a city right after the war started. But it hadn't changed or grown larger, but the idea would be to raise people's fighting spirit. There were a fish market, a police station, a fire station, a post office, a public bath, a temple, a shrine, a rice store, a cooking-oil store, and an elementary school. There was no hospital and no cars.

On September 1st, 1944, my sister and two brothers and I entered Urado National School. Since the war started, elementary school was called National School. Our school had first through eighth grade. One of our cousins, Sachiko, was an eighth grader; she looked more grown up to me than some adults and was precocious. All seventh and eighth grade students frightened me. On the first day I realized that we looked odd to all other students; my sister and I wore white silk, sailor's dresses, and my brothers were well dressed also. Sachiko gazed at us through thick glasses with an angry and surprised look. When we four kids were together and leaving the school, lots of students followed us. Some of them were shouting roughly, and running around us.

Sometime after we started school, about a hundred soldiers came and stayed at our school. They cooked at the lower ground and practiced military drill on the higher ground and spent nights in the classrooms.

Kids have talents about making nicknames. There was an officer whose nickname was Bamboo Holding Lieutenant; he was always holding a tiny bamboo stick and swinging and hitting at the air or earth. We were his friends because he seemed as young as our eighth grade students. When we shouted or called, "Bamboo Holding Lieutenant," he smiled and his face turned pretty red.

We students dug big pine tree stumps and roots out of the ground. Pine resin (pine tree gum) was used as oil for warships or warplanes, our teacher told us, and said, "Setsuko is the most persevering worker here." I felt glad.

At the house grandmother raised silk worms to make silk, so we picked mulberry leaves and ate mulberries for the first time. Our mouths were dyed purple. We were pointing at each other laughing. The berry's leaves didn't help our hunger, but the silkworms helped to make parachutes, mufflers, and flags of Japan.

The fish market was also changed. No longer were fish unloaded, but villagers came often there to see off the men called up to service in the military. The fish market was not a very large space, and near there was a jetty for cruising ships. Now even some remaining men in the village were drafted by the Japanese government to go to the war.

Ceremonies were held by all villagers in front of the fish market: women, kids, and remaining men, who were either old or in delicate health. Waiting for the drafted man, students made two lines, and everybody was holding a small paper flag of Japan.

Ceremonies went on regularly and formally.

A priest, an ex-soldier, was the representative of the villagers for the send off. His speech was boring, but his military uniform with many badges was very fancy to us because we only knew his priest's clothes. A "new soldier" made an address in reply. "Dear Everyone, thank you very much for coming to see me off even though you are so busy when I proceed to the front, I will make strenuous effort for our Country of Japan. I am prepared for death . . . and I will require your favor and our Country even though if only one ten thousands of it." Our heads were bowed and we listened to it very quietly; especially the boys were serious and quiet because next time will be their turn. They memorized the soldier's speech exactly because they would have to say it soon; they believed so.

"Now everybody," said the priest. "Have a *BANZAI* (cheers); would you let me lead a *BANZAI*, please." We shouted BANZAI three times.

Soon the new soldier was on the cruising ship, and the ship blew a whistle. BANZAI, BANZAI, we shouted loudly; the new soldier gave us salutes like a soldier. The ship left the jetty with the sound of the engine and whistles.

We shouldn't cry, so we didn't.

Booo, Booo, - - - the whistles and the ship became smaller and smaller; we were waving flags forever.

4. *Death*

One hot day a sad thing happened. A three year old boy didn't return home by the evening. The villagers searched for him and later he was found floating in the bay; he, Yasushi, was dead.

According to the village custom, he was laid on a board in front of his house. This was the first time I saw death. The mother was mad with grief, and the father was not there because he was away in the navy; he couldn't get home. While villagers were busy with the body or took care of their mother, Yasushi's nine year old brother disappeared. Obviously he suffered from Yasushi's death, and he felt guilty because older brothers and sisters almost always should take care of their younger sisters or brothers binding on their back.

Yasushi's funeral was next day. I never forgot the scene. Yasushi's sister followed the funeral procession, and I saw lice creeping on the nape of her neck.

At that moment I felt that hundreds of lice in my hair were running around trying to get out. The procession was going on to the graveyard. "Ne-chan," Misa-chan called me quietly and nodded; that meant I was okay. We felt very much ashamed that we had lice. I knew kids who were in the procession suffered lice both in the hair and on the body. The white lice on the body were tightly lined along every seam of our underwear. When we warmed a bit, they moved around and sucked our blood. We couldn't sleep in the winter.

We came to the graveyard where behind the pine trees and the open ocean, we prayed that Yasushi could sleep peacefully here, the most beautiful place in the village.

5. Bed Wetting

Soon my brothers, sisters, and I further lowered ourselves because we became bed (futon) wetters. We were frightened of the wet futon and the anticipated rebukes of our grandmother and aunts. By this time, another aunt came back from a big city, so we had three aunts and grandmother in the same house. I don't know why, but all of us became futon wetters. Later I often thought about it, but I didn't recognize the cause until recently. It was partly due to the big change caused by our evacuation to the fishing village during the war; we were shocked both mentally and physically. Now I can say the direct cause was the housing situation. My parents' house had two toilet rooms; one was for children's use and it was close to our bedroom. My grandmother's toilet was separated from main house although the roof covered the kitchen and toilet. The kitchen and toilet were half outside across an open hallway. Moreover, the house was built on the tall stone walls that rose directly from the sea water of the bay. These walls were twice as tall as an adult. At the ebb tide the whole foundation appeared, and at high tide the water nearly reached the house.

One night seven year old Nori-kun urinated in front of the kitchen, in the hallway, instead of into the sea because he went left from the main house. He was half asleep, and I think he was frightened of the dark sea and sky and the dark in the house, too. The toilet was right, sea side, from the main house, and there was not a urinal for men.

Our grandmother sentenced us to burn moxa, a medicinal herb, on our abdomens. She told us that moxa was good for our bed wetting. I had learned by this time that villagers used moxa as a punishment for kids.

We went into a panic. Literally we went to the dogs. We wandered as far from the house as we could do. We prayed night and day that the grandmother would change her mind, and we would not wet our futon. I felt that my whole body would be burned alive; it would be hell on earth.

The date of the punishment was announced. My sister, Misa-chan and I ran away together. We went into the mountains, our regular hiding place; soon my two brothers came. Nine year old brother Ma-kun had a burn mark from moxa because the grandmother had loved him and when he was three years old to six years old, he was adopted by the grandmother. Ma-kun showed us the mark, and said, "It's all right. I've had it since I was small, so . . . " Fu-chan didn't come, and I thought she was an exception because she was only five years old and the big aunt loved her. But she was not.

When I came near the house, I caught the sound, "No, no . . . forgive me . . . no . . . I never . . . please . . . forgive . . . " It was Fu-chan, crying. I ran into the house. At the entrance, the small aunt stood and forced me out and said, "You piss, damn! Do you want me to say to your teacher that you are a bed wetter?" I flinched from the fact and the difficulties. A quiet voice called me "Ne-chan." (dear sister!) from behind; it was Misa-chan. "Ne-chan, Ne-chan, ne, ne, ne . . . Humph, you are next!" I dashed into the house because I heard Fu-chan running around and crying. It meant punishment was over. "Fu-chan," I called up, she ran into my arms. From that time I became her "mother" until she died at fifteen years old.

Since that the grandmother and three aunts hated me, and I had hated them. Perhaps, developed as my habit, to think or to watch in these days. They had punished my two sisters and brothers. It was not in the same day, yet the punishment or moxa-treatment was not one time for one child. We each had several times when the wound scabbed and fell off; our grandmother waited for the next. We always felt pain because our shorts rubbed the wound, and a little blood came. So it was more painful than the first time.

The day came for my turn; I decided not to cry, but my teeth clicked in fear.

Suddenly my shorts were dragged down, and I trembled with shame. The grandmother laughed at me and said, "You bad girl, I give you favors." A moxa was on my skin, then, a burning joss stick ignited the moxa. It scorched my skin, but I could bear it. In fact, it was less painful than I thought. I moaned from physical pain and mental anguish, and I thought I had ten times moxa at the first time. Then, I realized that men's sounds were coming through an alley, and I knew who they were. I tried to pull up my shorts, but my arms were caught by the big aunt. Two aunts ran into the next room in a fluster. The sound of men's shoes stopped at a lattice window of the room where I laid. The punishments were carried on; I squeezed my eyes tight and my body became stiffened because of rejection. I caught a glimpse of them, but their half humble, oily, sweaty eyes were sticking fast on me. Why didn't I refuse them with all my strength?

Later I often thought about the cruel incident; it was imprinted on my mind, too. I understood that it was beyond my thought because of strong shock; I couldn't even think of my grandmother and aunts. I felt shamed and guilty; I felt I was a criminal.

I still have the mark; I never told anyone about the six eyes. My two aunts married two of them. My wounded vanity and my contempt for men were increased year by year either conscious or unconscious until I realized that I am getting older and don't have many more days and everybody will die.

6. *Our Country Was Burning*

I saw our country's break down; it was June, 1945. There was a city some thirty kilometers away from our village. When we were eating our supper, the shudder siren blew; next moment we were out of the house wearing thick hoods.

Bombers skimmed one after another; searchlights flashed. Soon bombing was started, and fire spread. Now the sky was also burnt beautifully. Pillars of fire shot up and sparked in the night. We couldn't hear the sounds, but across the bay the fire looked very close to our place. Unconsciously, we came out of the shelter, and stood as if rooted to the road. We had forgotten that it was very dangerous. How long did we stand motionless? Already a hint of the dawn or the reflection of the blaze showed on the windless surface of the bay.

We came to ourselves when our big aunt cried, "Let's have dinner, our last dinner." Her voice was excited or rather cheerful. "There are cans of fruit, dried fishes, and cube sugars. Eat all of them." But we could only eat a little food, silently.

I was urged by the silence. "Shall I laugh?" I said; ha, ha, ha, ha—ha, ha, ha . . . . Nori-kun laughed with me; Fu-chan came to me and laughed at me. Now five kids twisted our stomachs laughing and dancing.

Forty-one years passed.

Every summer reminds me of the time I stood by the open ocean, and now I understand what I was thinking that day. I was asking myself about the future, " . . . I came here, and where am I going . . . I lost everything . . . where are my parents, brother, and two little sisters?"

I couldn't get an answer because my future was white like a canvas where none of my future was written.

Setsuko's Comments

I came upon a poster for the Essay Contest in a dark, quiet corner of the school. It was at the end of summer vacation, a hot and very quiet day. The day reminded me of the summer of 1945, the period during our evacuation. Reading the poster, I felt all my cells quietly burning and heard the sounds of the ocean. The topic and title came in several minutes.

I wrote the essay little by little. Grammatical errors were corrected each time by the instructor, and I rewrote the paper. I had much trouble explaining Japanese habits and living during the war. I hope that my feelings are clear to the American reader.

I was a girl of twelve or thirteen when I was evacuated from my home in Nagasaki to the village where my grandmother and aunts lived. During World War II, the evacuation was shocking both physically and mentally.

When I got very sick several years ago, I didn't know why, but I often recalled my childhood, especially in my dreams. I recognized how the war and evacuation harmed my life and caused me to suffer a nervous breakdown.

The reward of writing this essay has been the relief of being able to express thoughts that have always been kept inside me. This writing is dedicated to my young sisters who died prematurely and anonymously as thousands of other children during World War II and the period of post war.

RELATIONSHIPS: PEOPLE

JESUS DE LA CRUZ
University of California, Davis
Terrence L. Dean, Instructor

Abandoned Friendship

Reflecting back at my childhood years, I can pinpoint experiences that have, through time, led me to a meaningful discovery of who I am. From an endless catalogue of these childhood experiences, my fondest memory, which so frequently comes to mind, is my relationship with Daniel. When I was four years old, my family came to reside in Whittier, California. The previous month had been very difficult, for my family had just completed a nerve-wracking and tiresome illegal immigration from Northern Mexico to sunny California. There were but a few Hispanic families residing in our residential area; luckily, a Hispanic family resided only two houses up our avenue. My sisters and I quickly became acquainted with the children of this family, enabling me, for the first time, to meet Daniel. Daniel was a normal Mexican-American child; physically, he had an adolescent body with its pot belly, undeveloped muscles and immature facial features. From our first encounter we would have never been able to comprehend the tremendous odyssey we would embark on, for our similarities would draw us closer together during our adolescent years. But our differences would ultimately force us to abandon our friendship.

Once I was acquainted with Daniel, we seemed inseparable, even though we occasionally got into some scuffles. We shared many similarities: we have the same last names although we are not related to one another. We were the same age, went to the same schools, and shared ideas and habits that were linked to what we liked to play, which was riding our Big Wheels. In no time at all, we were the best of friends. He did not associate as much with his friends, for they were insignificant now that we had each other. We would spend hours playing in my backyard, digging channels and tunnels to make a miniaturized delta. My mother knew when we were going to create something, for we would be racing in and out of the house readying the equipment. She didn't care much for what we did, but she would come outside and ask us what we would be doing. After we provided her with a brief answer, sometimes along with a little white lie, she would advise us of the precautions we would have to take. Satisfied that her advice was going to be taken seriously, she would go back into the house, knowing we would not be getting into too much trouble for a few hours. Once she left, we would commence the construction of our delta. Stolen silverware, which was smooched during our excursion into the house, was used to dig into the soil. We would work diligently and with great precision; we created a network of channels and tunnels where water could run as it irrigated my mother's flower bed. The day seemed to go too fast, for we would find ourselves still adding additional channels to our delta, when we heard my mother calling for dinner. During this time, with everything that I was able to experience, Daniel had the same or similar experience mainly because we were constantly together.

Since Daniel and I resided a few houses away from one another, we experienced a very similar or almost identical exposure to our environment. Our experiences together helped us form our moral standards which would last our entire lives. Our first experience in learning what adults could do and children were forbidden to do took place when we decided to start smoking. My sister introduced us to cigarettes while we were playing in our clubhouse secretly located in our cellar. Daniel was able to pick up smoking quite rapidly; I, on the other hand, coughed throughout the whole experience. Fortunately for me, for I would probably have died of all the coughing, someone saw us smoking and snitched on us. Our mothers were furious over our behavior and disciplined us until their arms hurt. Whether we were experiencing good or bad situations, Daniel and I were experiencing our environment together.

Unfortunately, as Daniel and I grew out of our adolescence, we began to drift apart. Our environment that seemed so identical in our adolescence slowly evolved to a point where we lived at opposite ends of a spectrum. He reacquainted himself with his old friends and, like a friend, I followed him. I was astonished by the way Daniel's attitude changed while we were with his friends. I suspect it was the environment that had changed him so rapidly, for we would always find ourselves in abandoned garages and alleys, talking about sex or other topics which we had yet to experience. I couldn't fit into this environment, for I did not know what to talk about and felt forced to participate in criminal games, so we saw less and less of one another as each year passed, and finally, for some reason, we would avoid meeting each other at all. I don't know why Daniel began to dislike me, but I do know he did and still does. I can remember that in fifth grade we had stopped hanging around one another. I still considered him my friend, but he didn't want my friendship, for he had other more important friends. When I looked at him, sitting a few lunch tables away from me, I could see the hatred in his eyes concentrating on me; his eyebrows would become intense as his face became solid and heartless. Somewhere we lost one another, and now it was too late to try to find our adolescent friendship.

I was aware of only one slight difference in Daniel's and my characters, and that was that Daniel had the ability to be more socially outgoing while I was aware of myself and the importance I played in my environment; as a result, I had a difficult time in showing who I was. I remember during the sixth grade, I was characterized by my peers as being mature for my age. I did not see myself as a mature person. Instead I saw myself as being less skillful than my schoolmates, for I lacked academic skills and tended to work by myself. One bright sunny day, a group of girls decided to create a family at school, I was sitting on the grass enjoying the sun with my legs crossed and my hands underneath my chin, watching a bee pollinate clovers, when a group of girls came by and stood around me. I heard one of them scream and then saw the bee crushed to death by a girl's shoe. I looked up and smiled as I greeted them. "Would you like to be our father?" one of them asked, and I, without thinking said, "Yes." Later that day, I found out that Daniel was going to marry one of my daughters. He came up to me and asked if he could marry Gina; I replied, "Yes" without any further thought on the matter. But while looking at Daniel, with his face lit and smiling, I thought to myself "He has forgotten that he hates me." Without any further exchange of words, he left, leaving me to wonder if he had found what he was looking for in life.

Daniel was sucked up into his social environment which eventually drove him to drop out of high school, and then he simply disappeared from sight. I was briefly reacquainted with him during a party after some years of not knowing his whereabouts. My friends and I were sitting on a curb drinking beer and listening to music when I saw Daniel walking up the street. Physically he had matured: he didn't have his pot belly, his shoulders were wider, and his facial features somehow had deteriorated since I last saw him. As he came closer, I noticed he was wearing baggy pants and that his hair was greased and combed straight back. At this time, one of my friends spotted him and stood up to greet him. My heart stopped, for I did not know what to expect. I looked at him while he was greeting my friends and noticed he was under the influence of drugs. I could tell he was ignoring me, for he dreaded the moment he would have to greet me. He greeted my friends with a Cholo style handshake; I could never remember how those handshakes worked. Now, I was the only one he had to greet. I could not face him as I used to in my adolescent years, so I stretched out my hand and forced myself to look at him. He didn't want to make eye contact, so he quickly tilted his head down. I was expecting a Cholo handshake, but instead I felt a firm grip. I immediately felt a surge of energy flow through us, overwhelming both of us, forcing us to break apart. Without exchanging any words, we both had a glimpse into each other's feelings. What I saw was a friend, very distant and chained to his environment and its expectations.

Reflecting back on my relationship with Daniel, I wonder if we could have somehow overcome our differences and stayed friends. I wish we could have, for then I would have been an extension of him, with the ability to have some insight into who he was and how he interpreted our experiences. I find myself asking why our relationship was abandoned. Maybe our similarities were not strong enough and our differences separated us far enough, so that we wanted to forget that we were once friends. Or did I mature too fast, leaving him behind with disillusionment and not wanting to catch up? One thing I am sure of, and that is I want to talk to him. Maybe someday?

Jesus' Comments

There is a short story written by Rushworth M. Kidder called "Depth on the Surface" in which Kidder reconstructs a childhood memory. From this piece of writing I obtained the generalization of a person's look at a childhood memory and forged my own short story.

I spent a week carefully analyzing the content of what would be my first draft. The first days of the week were spent on reconstructing the evolution of Daniel's and my friendship. I had to go back and organize my memories in a chronological order and then edited the sum of memories into an organized and accurate account of our friendship. Thus, my first draft was able to give a substantial account of my first acquaintance with Daniel to our last encounter. Because of my own extensive editing, before writing the first draft, my only concern about rewriting was to focus in on the relationship.

My greatest problem in writing the paper turned out to be my greatest reward. Editing was my major problem in writing the paper, for I tried to focus as well as develop the relationship I had with Daniel. Meanwhile, my constant flashbacks into adolescence let me rediscover my adolescence, which was filled with joy and happiness. In addition, it let me reflect on the feeling I experienced while my relationship with Daniel was gradually crumbling apart.

LORRAINE FOGG
University of Northern Colorado
Phyllis S. Endicott, Instructor

Staying Tough

When I was a little girl, I would draw my father pictures of animals and houses. When I was done, I would run up and ask, "Do you like it, Daddy? Do you like it?" Sometimes he would be so busy he wouldn't hear me. Other times he would make such a big deal out of my Crayola picture that I felt on top of the world. As I got older, I looked for his approval in other ways, such as in my grades in school or in the boyfriends I chose. Throughout my life, I have looked for my father's approval in everything I've done.

My father died of cancer two years ago, and I still miss him very much. I miss so many things about him: his sense of humor, his smile, and his blue eyes that could look right through me. But most of all I miss talking to him. So many things have happened to me in the past few years that I would like to talk to him about. I have experienced a divorce, started school, and done a lot of growing up. I often wonder if he would approve of the things that have happened since his death. I guess I still need to know that he's proud of me and what I've done with my life.

One night I had a very strange dream that involved my father. I was at my parents' house visiting my mom and dad. My father was well and sitting in his favorite chair at the dining room table. He was wearing the baseball cap he used to always wear when he worked in his garden, and he was visiting with my boyfriend, Mark, who dad actually never met. My father looked so happy. Suddenly, he got up from the table and went to his room. When he came out he no longer had on the baseball cap and was wearing pajamas. He was very thin and ill. His skin was yellow from a dying liver, just as it was when he was in the hospital before his death. He sat down at the table and said, "I'm going to die." I started to cry, shaking my head, not wanting to hear what he was saying. He then said, "I'm proud of you, Lori. You'll make it just fine without me. Be tough!" Then I woke up. This was the only dream I've had of my father since his death.

I have always felt that I never completely accepted my father's death. My mother and brother always felt that I would fall apart when my father died because of the special relationship that I had with him. When I was called to the hospital, in the last few days of my father's life, my mother had a priest waiting for me just in case I became too emotional. I was determined to show them that I was tough and would not fall apart. Throughout that terrible time of my father's death and funeral I was the tough one, the one that everyone leaned on. The terrible thing was that I was so busy being tough that I never got the chance to realize that my daddy was gone. Suddenly, it hit me that I had to learn to live without him.

I feel that the dream helped me to accept the fact that my father is gone. Time will also help me to deal with my loss and learn to live with it. Eventually, I feel that I will be able to think back on my father and smile, for no one can take my memories away. The dream also made me realize that, just as I did as a little girl with my drawings, I am still looking for my father's approval. Somehow, through this dream I feel that I have received it.

Lorraine's Comments

This paper started out as a dream one night and has evolved, through revising and soul searching, into this essay. The first version started out as a diagnostic, in-class timed writing, at the start of the fall quarter, in my English 120 class. We got a choice of topics to write about, and I chose "My Greatest Dream." The topic was easy for me to write on, for I had just had a dream about my father a week before. When the time was up, I found that I still had a lot to say. The next assignment given to me by my instructor was to write a narrative that made a point, so I decided to continue with the story of my dream. After writing the paragraph, I felt that I still had much to say. The next assignment we were given was to expand our paragraph into an essay. I finally had the chance to express my feelings more fully and expand the story of my dream, and yet I was stuck. I felt as though I had a lot of feelings about my father and his death tucked away inside of me, but I didn't know how to let them out. One night I decided to do some revising at the computer lab on the Apple IIe, using the Bank Street Writer. I sat there for over thirty minutes, staring at the screen, trying to decide how to revise and add on to my paper when suddenly an idea came to me. I started to write and added on a whole new paragraph, paragraph number four, which deals with what I went through at the time of my father's death. In writing my paper, I realized that I had never accepted my father's death and writing this paper was the first step toward accepting it. I have now written out my feelings and have been forced to look at them. Thanks to this essay, I am well on my way in getting over the pain of losing my father.

DAVID A. REED
Owens Technical College (Ohio)
Dorothy S. Bonser, Instructor

I.

To the ten-year-old boy, the treasures that lay within the red leather box were truly magical and mystical. With the lid wide open the boy stood mystified as he looked through the collection of broken lighters, paper clips, screws, buttons, and other valuable items. It must have taken his father years to accumulate such a mass of wealth, he thought. In a tray that popped up when the lid was open lay a bandless watch that was missing the minute hand and one cufflink with the initial F engraved on it. The box smelled sweet probably because there was a half a roll of Tums, two or three Lifesavers without wrappers, and a cigar with "IT'S A BOY" marked on it. A small metal lapel pin that had the words "I LIKE IKE" printed on it was stuck into the side of the box. Bound in a rubberband and neatly tucked in the flap of the lid were several pictures of a skinny, brown-eyed boy with a butch haircut, probably too precious to throw away. Just as he was about to close the lid, the finest treasure of all caught his eye. It was a ballpoint pen with a picture of a girl in a black bathing suit on the side. When the pen was turned upside down, the bathing suit disappeared, and a naked lady was revealed.

II.

While visiting my father recently, I suddenly realized how the years have brought about a reversal of roles in our relationship. He brought out a digital watch that I had given him and asked me to set it for him. As I sat at the kitchen table setting the watch, memories of the past stirred within me. It must have been about twenty-five years ago, in that very same kitchen, that I came to him with my most treasured possession, a Hoppalong Cassidy wristwatch. Somehow the minute hand had fallen off and was lying at the bottom of the crystal. I watched in amazement as my father, with the skills of a surgeon, dissected the watch and had it good as new within ten minutes. Twenty-five years ago I thought he was a mechanical genius, there wasn't a thing around that he couldn't repair or build. I depended on his knowledge in many ways as I was growing up. Back then the one thing I figured he didn't know was how to enjoy life. He was too busy working and raising a family. I, on the other hand, knew how to enjoy life. I was busy playing with my friends, riding my bike, and having fun. Now, twenty-five years later, our roles are reversed. He depends on me for my mechanical knowledge, and I depend on him for his knowledge of life.

David's Comments

In both of the assignments I found that I had many thoughts that I felt would be interesting to my reader. Linking these short choppy thoughts into smooth homogeneous sentences that were related to each other was my most difficult task. I made most of my changes by reading and rereading what I had written, listening to my ear every time. Then I would refine what I had just read and repeat the process until I was fully satisfied. In both of my paragraphs the greatest reward was knowing that a little of what is in my heart will bring some joy or a smile to my reader.

STEPHEN R. MITCHELL
Kent State University, Salem Campus (Ohio)
Nancy McCracken, Instructor

Dear Grandma,

Remember the summers I spent with you and Grandpa down on the farm? I'll never forget the wonderful times I had. I don't think any young boy could have received a better example of love and understanding than you and Grandpa showed me. I know, it's been a long time but I never got the chance to tell you what it really meant to me. It's etched in my mind like a footprint in the fresh snow.

I can still remember sitting in second grade, my mind wandering to the summer vacation that was a few weeks away and thinking about all the good times I'd had on the farm in West Virginia. Even though it's been almost twenty years since the good Lord took Grandpa, I can still picture him standing in his tobacco shed, with his old, tattered, sweat laden straw hat, dirty bib-overalls, and manure covered boots, admiring his crop with a gleam in his eyes that showed how proud he really was. I still think of the times when after a hard day's work in the tobacco fields, we sat on the front porch: Grandpa in his rocking chair, with his hat tilted back, showing his snow white forehead, chewing on a big wad of tobacco, and telling me stories of the good old days.

Grandma, do you recall the times that he would take me to the barn to harness up Molly and Bill, his two work horses? I can still smell the old leather that was in the barn, and hear how he would ask me in his hillbilly drawl, "Which one you wanta ride today, Stevie?" Then he would grab me with his big, strong, calloused hands and swing me up on one of their backs. I would hold on to the harness horns for dear life, as he would give the commands that the horses knew so well. I could never figure out how, but those horses would seem to know what he was saying. Whenever he would yell "gee" they turned left, and for "haw" they turned right. He always told me, "These here are the best damn team of horses in these hills," and I knew he was right.

I think one of the best times that I can recollect was when we made apple butter. You had told me, during the week, that come Saturday we were going to have a big day. And a few days later, Grandpa got the huge, black, iron kettle out and started a fire underneath it. Folks came from miles around and from every direction. I still remember sitting, listening to the old timers tell their stories, and the smell of apple butter filling the evening air. I couldn't believe how many people were there. The men folk, with cob pipes, chewing tobacco and drinking from little brown jugs, seemed so happy and content. Those were the best of times, and I know that those people didn't have a lot of money, but they stood together and helped each other. I learned that folks helping each other was a way of life then, but that type of closeness is all but gone now.

Yes Grandma, the memories are as clear as the water that we hand pumped from the old well: the rooster crowing in the early morning hours, the little white farm house, nestled in the hills, with its old wood cook-stove that filled the early morning with the smell of fresh baked biscuits, and the sound of burning, popping wood, mixed in with the crackling of bacon and eggs. I remember you standing by the stove with your long dress and apron, telling me to go wash up, for breakfast was almost ready. I would hurriedly do so, knowing that when I returned to the big oak table there would be a feast fit for a king.

As my mind wanders back to that little white farmhouse, Grandpa's rocking chair, the swing on the front porch, the little red barn that sat down the gravel road, with its infamous "Chew Mailpouch Tobacco" painted on its side, I realized the values I learned as a seven year old. Grandma, I could never begin to repay you and Grandpa for the lessons I learned on that farm as a young boy. All the times you made me wash behind my ears, say grace at the supper table, and respect my elders are still with me even today. Grandma, thank you for the wonderful times on that little tobacco farm. Thank you for the love, understanding, and gentle discipline. Thank you for being Grandma, in every sense of the word, for this I do know: you *both* will receive a just reward, like nothing on this earth.

Your Loving Grandson,
Steve

Steve's Comments

When I first started thinking of who I was going to write a letter to my first thoughts were of Mom or Dad. As I sat at the kitchen table thinking about what to write, I started speculating about my Grandmother and wondering how she was. My Grandmother is ninety-eight years old and now resides in a nursing home in Canton, Ohio. She's not in very good health, and her mind is to the point when she didn't know who I was the last time I saw her. This really hurt me because we were so close. So I decided to write her a letter and tell her all the things that I never really told her years ago. As the words flowed from my pen to the paper, I realized that I was writing a testimonial to her. All the memories came back to me as if they only happened yesterday. My greatest pleasure was reading the essay in class and letting everyone know what a kind and terrific person she really is. This writing assignment I thought would be difficult but as it turned out it was a real pleasure. I made very few changes in my drafts, except spelling and punctuation. The essay came from my feelings for her, so therefore required very little editing.

STEVE SHAVER
The University of Akron (Ohio)
Jim Sollisch, Instructor

Hidden Bitterness

I was born in the country, but I am presently living in Akron, Ohio while attending college. It is sometimes difficult adjusting from corn fields and dirt roads to towering skyscrapers and four lane highways through town. But the hardest thing I have found trouble adjusting to so far is the hidden bitterness in many of the people walking on the streets. I think the media has a lot to do with why people are sometimes afraid of their fellow human beings, because all they like to talk about on the news anymore are all the bad things people are doing, which in turn is bound to make people leery. But what really left an indelible impression with me was seeing such an act of violence in person with my own two eyes. My roommate and I were downtown in the Cascade Plaza on a gloomy, dreary day in early fall. After paying our gas bill we were walking around in the courtyard minding our own business. As we were heading to our car our attention was focused on a boy who looked to be in his teens. The boy was wearing a tattered leather coat that looked to be about three sizes too big, a pair of worn out "nike" hightops, and a holey pair of levis. He was riding a red motor-cross bicycle skillfully on the crowded lunch hour street as he approached an elderly woman. She appeared to be no more than a bag lady who was wearing very old, worn out tennis shoes, a coat that looked to be an army jacket that had actually been through a war, and a knit hat which was pulled down over her ears revealing her dirty face. She was pulling a little cart which was full of groceries that could very well have been all she owned. The boy followed the lady for a couple of minutes. Suddenly he produced a cunning grin and look of determination on his face. Then he gradually picked up speed, gracefully dodging people as he approached the lady, kicking the cart with his left foot, knocking it and the old lady over with a thud. As this poor old lady's groceries rolled everywhere, that little bastard rode away laughing, yelling back at her to ask her if it was her first day on new legs. As if that wasn't bad enough, there were people practically tripping over this poor old woman as she lay helpless on the ground, but no one would stop and help her. By the time we got over to her, she was trying to get up, looking like a new born fawn trying to get to her feet on wobbly legs. I put my hand under her shoulder to help her to her feet, and she instantly went into a panic stricken rage because she was afraid that I was going to rob her. While assuring her that all we wanted to do was help, I got her to sit on a bench and relax a little bit, as my roommate, Steve Herbert, was picking up the groceries that people had kicked all over the place. I can still see the Campbell Soup can rolling down the street.

That day was a first for myself and Jean, the old lady. It was a first for Jean because she said it was the first time in many years that she can remember someone other than a family member wanting to help her without wanting something in return. It was also a first for me because I had never been in downtown Akron before and to be honest I was not impressed.

RELATIONSHIPS: PLACES & THINGS

LUE ANN DEVENY
West Virginia State College
Diana Wohl, Instructor

Neatly tucked away in the small, drab presence of my laundry room is an old-fashioned, pullout, square-framed window. I think this is my favorite spot, speaking a language understandable only to me. It stands just above my dutiful washer and dryer behind my constant supply of laundry detergent. Because of its crusted layers of white paint and its squeaky, brass turning lock, a design of forgotten workmanship, this window looks as if it has witnessed other lifetimes. To me this old relic is a picture frame with an ever changing portrait.

Over the steep hillside, across a peaceful field, trailing over a timid creek, just above a mysterious maze of a forest, out beyond the horizon, I see the pastel sky of my much-anticipated, morning sunrise anxiously pulling me into the new day, for this window is the first thing I see as I hesitantly scuffle through the laundry room on my way to the bathroom for morning rituals.

Afternoons of routine work and drudgery are quickly relieved as my window, a welcome reprieve, interrupts meaningless, ungrateful repetition by sharing one, brief, momentary feeling of serenity and renewal as the brightness of midday lifts my tired eyes toward my window.

Evenings are not so kind. The cruel darkness slowly steals the spiritually uplifting path of life-giving light from my window, leaving me with feelings of regret, not having cherished it enough.

On occasion I'm drawn to this window by the pungent, crisp smell of rain. Taking my front row, theatre seat, I anxiously await the upcoming performance. Thick lines of seething, black clouds fight the sky for a prevailing rain as they clamor on the tree-lined horizon.

Outside the window, the changing seasons each create their own unique painting. Spring brings an exciting view of wet, black bark. Trees come alive with lime green buds as my hillside gently unfolds with daffodils.

Summer's portrait is peaceful and quiet: a thick, green, velvety blanket of swaying trees accompanied by the constant buzz of the nearby bees. The window, which now remains open, is a lifeline for the rationed, sweet breezes of summer.

I think fall is my favorite season. Delighting in the musky smell of leaves, I look out over the hillside at fields of mustard yellow golden rod laced with brown, crackly cat-tails. The trees all around are aglow with the dazzling colors of autumn: watermelon red, lemon yellow, pumpkin orange, chestnut brown. Nature's skilled brush has painted a masterpiece unveiled for a brief, first and final show, receiving my undivided attention several times a day.

At last my sleepy, winter portrait has arrived. Depleted of life, my hillside is laid to rest, disappearing under a protective blanket. Every crack and crevice of the bare trees are carefully dusted with a fine glistening powder, taking on the appearance of pedestals, proudly displaying heaven's most exquisite gift.

Each year the art work of my window is more beautiful than the one before. The window, as if holding the wisdom of its age, expertly and lovingly cradles the tender pictures that are born there, live there, only briefly, and die there ever so gracefully. I feel as if this window was placed in my little laundry room for my own sole purposes of strength and enjoyment. This is not just a window, it is a gallery filled with my private thoughts, feelings, and treasures.

Lue Ann's Comments

My paper started as an assignment to write a descriptive paper about a favorite person or place. I chose to write about my laundry room window because of its unique appearance. I've always thought that a laundry room was an odd place for a window with such a beautiful view.

As I revised my paper, I used the sentence combining skills that were taught in class, making my writing better and more explanatory. After deciding to revise my paper for the contest, I would jot down ideas that I had been going over in my mind whenever I had a spare moment.

Being given the opportunity to express myself and then having it considered good enough to enter a contest was my greatest, most motivating reward in undertaking this project.

SHIRLEY J. NORRIS
State Technical Institute of Memphis (Tennessee)
Barbara C. Baxter, Instructor

Unto These Hills

Notable people have been inspired to compose songs, paint pictures or write books, all paying homage to their hometowns. And there are those, like myself, who just like to reminisce about childhood days in a small town. The thoughts that fill my head now, and always leave a yearning to return to Unicoi County, Tennessee, are the splendors of the four seasons. God really outdid Himself in this tiny area that is sheltered by the Great Smokey Mountains.

In winter the largest snowflakes anyone has ever seen fell like feathers from the sky. The snow was pure and clean, as the saying goes. We never worried about pollution when making snow creme. The snow didn't fall far enough from the heavens to gather any harmful chemicals before it reached us.

Frozen pipes weren't any problem, because there was no inside water. Water was carried from a natural spring, located several hundred feet from the house, down a steep incline. Carrying water was the children's duty. It wasn't a job, but instead a great tobogganing ride, without a sled. We simply sat on the cushion of snow, and given a push, would slide to the bottom. The trick was carrying the full pail to the top of the slope. My sisters and I would station ourselves, as in a relay, the first one slipping and sliding back to the top to retrieve the now half full bucket of water.

Spring was a tonic. It wasn't bitter, as tonics can be, but a cleansing ritual. The ground was now clean and vibrant for planting. Ole Contrary, the plowing mule, must have been the only one who didn't like to see spring. But once he was harnessed and the plow bit into the spongy earth, the smell must have been like an elixir. If the blinders weren't on, he would occasionally swing his mammoth head around to see us breaking the dirt clods, and as if to say, "Are you keeping up with me?" Spring was just what God ordered after the winter.

Summers in these rocky mountains would be hot. Just as it seemed we were closer to the snowflakes, so it was with the sun. It would come up earlier and be hotter than anywhere else. After helping Ole Contrary with the plowing and weeding, the creek was the place for us. Now if the sun was hot, the creek was the Arctic. Hot and tired as we were, modesty never was a question. Stripping down to our feed sack bloomers, there was a dare and dread of hitting this icy water. Being a rotten egg never bothered me. I would hesitantly enter the water. Carefully stepping on the slick creek rocks, I would gradually become accustomed to the cold. My delicate entry would end when someone would pull me under and swim back to the deep part, called Devil's Hole. Goose fleshed, teeth chattering, and blue from the cold, we emerged to let the sun cradle us in its now pleasant warmth.

As summer's strength slipped, my favorite season gradually appeared—autumn. It was a final hallelujah to God's handiwork. A time for reverence and thanksgiving. The trees of scarlet, orange, russet, and gold, polkadotted the mountainsides. The chilly early mornings caused the chimney smoke to cut a path through the blue gray haze. Wanting to snuggle a moment longer between the goose down mattress and comforter, we would smell the potato yeast biscuits and fresh apple butter (the real thing) and growling tummies dashed for the round kitchen table. The smokehouse was being filled with inventory of delicacies canned in a #2 washtub on a wood stove. The quilt squares, from flour and feed sacks, were waiting for creation, for the coming winter. The Sunday dinner chicken feathers, all washed in rain water, were waiting for new ticking to pillow a tired, sleepy head. It was the final soliloquy. Autumn seemed to say, "It's time to prepare for resting the body and soul. You can enjoy in retrospect."

So with Big Ben ticking away on the fireplace mantel, winters were joyful. Spring serenaded us with rain on the tin roof and in the summer the rhododendron scented our world. And in autumn, the whip-o-wills called out "Good Night to all in Unicoi County, Tennessee."

Shirley's Comments

The subject assigned in my developmental writing course was "hometown life and the benefits of a small community." With encouragement and expert advice from my instructor, I revised the original thought with the help of pictures taken of Unicoi County. The initial changes included spelling corrections and more picturesque phrases to better describe what I felt.

The process of repeated revisions filled me with a sense of accomplishment and encouragement.

JOE ADAMS
Los Angeles Pierce College (California)
Harriet Fellner, Instructor

The Blind Chicken

The blind chicken nests alone as the other hens walk in and out of the open coop. The blind bird sits in a corner as if she is incubating some imaginary egg. The other hens seem to pay no attention to her unless she gets in their way. Then they'll peck at her and walk away.

Each day I see this sightless hen's body withering away regardless of the countless days that I spend holding a can of chicken scratch in front of her beak. As I stand outside the coop and watch her when she gets hungry, she goes to the free feed bucket out of habit, which holds the feed. She will peck at the ground or hit her face on the side of the bucket trying to get at the food.

The lack of sight keeps her down when she is hungry or thirsty; as a result, she is losing weight and growing weaker by the day. If this blind bird has more energy than is required for sustaining life, she is not showing it. She doesn't go for water as often as she should, nor is she eating as often as the other hens.

The hen's feathers are dry and falling off, as dead leaves would fall off a dead tree, floating helplessly to the ground. I've watched this bird that became blind from some unknown trauma go from a normal, healthy state to a mal-nourished lump of feathers lying on the ground. She went from the top of the pecking order to a helpless pecking bag for the other hens.

Joe's Comments

I was at a loss as to what to write about when I thought about the chicken that I was trying to keep alive and decided to write about her. My first draft was more narrative than descriptive, so I changed parts to be more descriptive.

My main problem was figuring out what to write about.

The greatest reward for me is knowing that someone besides myself actually liked something that I have written.

MIKE QUINLAN
Mallinckrodt College (Illinois)
Sr. Marie Saffert, Instructor

Another One Bites the Dust

When one hears the name Porsche, the first thing that comes to mind is a vision of an unearthly fast, sleek, super sports car with no equal. The mere mention of the name Porsche in front of a gang of pseudo-automobile experts will have them oo-ing and ah-ing with wagging tongues. Furthermore, these onion heads will be blindly praising an overinflated name. Most likely they know little or nothing about the Porsche automobile line.

Why do people have such high praise, deep respect, and total awe for a car line that is nothing but rolling garbage? Television and the movies are largely responsible for filling people's heads with overinflated images. The producers of such films are grossly technically inaccurate, often showing a Porsche outrunning just about anything short of the space shuttle. This technical inaccuracy is in the same light as the old B grade Westerns that show "six shooters" firing twenty times without reloading.

One day while waiting at the stoplights in my 450 horsepower 302W Cobra II, a new Ruff 911 Turbo pulled up next to me. The left lane the Porsche was in merged into mine about 1200 feet down. The middle-aged man in the Porsche revved his motor and slowly inched up, clearly a challenge and test to my Cobra II. A Turbo 911 would blow most stock Cobra II's away, but the fool did not realize what he was getting himself into. As the 911 got through revving its motor, it was only proper to return the call. The man's face changed from a confident and sure look to one of ghastly fear when he heard a blueprinted tunnel-rammed 302W crank out 450 plus horsepower through open headers.

The light was soon to go green. Both cars continued to inch forward while bringing the revs of both cars in the 6000 RPM range. Suddenly the light turned green. Both accelerators floored, tires screeching and laying rubber took off neck and neck; but as my motor hit the midrange, it was all over for the man in the $60,000 Porsche. A $6,000 1978 Ford Cobra II had blown his turbocharged wonder machine away by two bus lengths.

Mike's Comments

I chose my topic, automobiles, because of my long-time interest in them. I had almost four months of rigorous in-depth practice in all aspects of writing. On this specific paper, I spent many hours on revisions, editing, and research. To select a topic for the contest, I recalled an event that actually happened.

UNEXPECTED OUTCOMES

MIKE GREENE
California State University, Fresno
David R.C. Good, Instructor

Don't Shoot the Piano Player

Never judge a book by its cover. I'd heard it a thousand times before, but it had never rung as true as it did that rainy Easter Sunday twelve years ago.

It has been a tradition in my family, for more than a few generations, to begin the holiday drinking early in the day. Not wanting to be the first to break with tradition, I awoke early and began preparing myself for an arduous day of bar duty. The routine was the same. I'd call Charlie, my oldest friend and confidant; we would find a watering hole and begin our vigil.

I heard Charlie's car pull up, and I ran outside into the early morning drizzle. Charlie worked for a used car dealership and always had a "like new" set of wheels for us to carouse in. This time was no exception, a shiny new, (or fairly new) 1973 green, four door Lincoln Continental.

We stopped at one of the "stop-n-robs" by my apartment and picked up a cold sixer of Coors beer. As we pulled away from the store, I leaned back in the seat, popped the top, looked over at Charlie and said, "Where to?"

"The nearest cocktail lounge," he said grinning. We headed south on Blackstone Avenue. The rain was really starting to come down, and the sound of water splashing under the wheels nearly drowned out the sound of the radio. Both of us were a little put out by the fact that all the bars were closed, and we had nowhere to go. I was about to suggest that we go back to my apartment, when I glanced to my right and noticed an "Open" sign in the window of a small tavern. We turned the car around and pulled into the flooded parking lot.

Dee's 41 Club was nestled between an adult bookstore and an auto supply outlet. Dee's was the only bar left in this old neighborhood of rundown houses and small shops. It had the appearance of a place whose time had come and gone. Even the graffiti on the peeling exterior was dated.

We parked the car and walked inside. Smoke hung in thick clouds around imitation Tiffany lamps that lit the shuffleboard and pool tables that were to our right. Directly in front of us and extending to the left was the bar. Seated at the bar was the oddest assortment of characters I'd seen in some time. They were reminiscing about what Dee's had been before the rich walnut paneling was painted over with a dismal off white enamel.

One old boy at the bar told a story about the night two of the Brooklyn Dodgers, their names now obscured by the time and drink, won all the money in a shuffleboard tournament, only to lose it back to Pinkey something-or-other at the pool tables.

"I met my first husband right over there," said a buxom, beehive brunette in her mid-fifties, pointing to the pool tables. She radiated with a mature sensuality, despite the smell of the whiskey and beer she was sipping.

"When I lost him in 66, we held the wake right here. I think Dee had sold the place then." Her eyes wandered briefly. "Hell, I can't remember that far back."

I leaned over the torn padding on the bar and asked the bartender for change for the jukebox.

"Doesn't work," he said flatly. "There's an upright behind you, if you think you can handle it." A wide grin swept across his face.

I walked over and sat down on two milk crates that were being used for a piano stool. "What do you want to hear?" I asked Charlie.

"Chopsticks," he said.

"Too hard. Something a little easier maybe."

"Get me a gun," he said sarcastically.

"He probably don't know that one either," chuckled the bartender.

I began playing the only thing I know, the intro to "Let It Be."

"Don't shoot the piano player," I heard a voice say. I looked up and saw a short stocky man in a pair of cover-alls and a Sinclair Paint cap moving toward me. He was about sixty-five or seventy years old with pale blue eyes and about a week's growth of beard.

"Those black keys are there for a reason. You gotta hit em once in a while." He came around the piano where I was seated and edged me off the milk crates as he leaned in to demonstrate.

"Care to have a go at it?" I asked. He settled on to the milk crates and adjusted his weight, leaning forward just a little. I noticed he had the hands of a working man and not a musician. Hands that were chapped, the skin cracked and dried, the fingers muscled and thick from years of gripping rollers and paint brushes.

"Anything in particular you'd like to hear, young fella?" he asked.

"How about 'Somewhere Over the Rainbow,' or 'Moon River,'" I said, half expecting to be told he didn't know it.

With that he broke into one of those chromatic hammer-on scales like Floyd Cramer is famous for and then straight into one of the most beautiful renditions of "Over the Rainbow" I had ever heard. When he finished "Over the Rainbow" he moved on through the forties, fifties, and sixties. The buxomy brunette came down and belted out a truly original version of "Easter Parade." I remember thinking how funny a bonnet would have looked on that beehive hairdo. We sang and drank, about eight or ten of us, until about nine that night.

The old piano player talked about his days as a honky tonk man during the prohibition era in mob run Chicago. He had played for Capone and the boys and met most of the celebrities that had come through town. When the forties hit, circumstances had forced him to retire the piano and go in search of a more lucrative vocation. All those years of talent went unused—unused maybe, but not wasted.

I don't know about Charlie, but I will carry the memory of that day with me for a long, long time—the memory of the day that an old man in funny clothes sat down behind the keys of an old Baldwin Upright piano and turned a cold rainy Easter into an unforgettable memory.

Mike's Comments

Years ago I heard an author on television describing his approach to writing. He said he sat at his typewriter until beads of blood formed on his forehead. So far I guess I've been lucky; the beads on my forehead have been sweat and not blood, but I understood what he meant.

We were asked in my English class to write about a holiday memory. I thought about the topic most of the weekend, and it wasn't until Sunday evening that I remembered the old piano player. I began writing immediately, right off the top of my head. I have to have complete solitude when I'm trying to gather my thoughts and put them on paper. The phone rang several times, and my girlfriend insisted I look at some clothes she'd bought, so my first draft ended up being more of an outline.

The next day I began to connect all the pieces of the outline. My second draft was a little out of sequence. I tried to recall the day in which the story took place. I found myself injecting opinions into the story that weren't formed until later. I think this is a common problem with many movie writers, this tendency to give opinion rather than show the reader what it is the writer is trying to convey.

The story of the piano player is truer and it is a pleasant memory, but the true joy of putting it down on paper comes in the understanding and acceptance of who I was then and who I am now.

KEVIN E. LARCHER
State Technical Institute at Knoxville (Tennessee)
Eleanor R. Stiles, Instructor

My Summer Job: A Pleasant Fate

All I really wanted was an easy, part-time job during my summer vacation. I deserved a break. After all, since the age of thirteen, I had worked long and hard as an apprentice carpenter. Consequently, after three years without a vacation, I had decided that I had earned a summer of rest and relaxation. My parents, on the other hand, had their own plans for me. They persuaded me to accept a carpentry job that my Aunt Dana said was available in Nevada. My fate was sealed. I was soon having nightmarish visions of driving across the country to find myself in the middle of a dry, dusty, desert wasteland, under a bright blistering sun, buzzards circling overhead, waiting for me—their next meal. However, not until I arrived on the job, did I find that I would be working at Lake Tahoe. In spite of my fears, it was to be one of the best jobs I've ever had. My job sites were breathtakingly beautiful, and my work was surprisingly enjoyable.

Just the opportunity of being able to soak up the incredible beauty of the Lake Tahoe area was nearly payment enough for me. Indeed, there were many times that I seemed to forget I was working. Sometimes, during a break, I found a lofty perch to look out over the magnificent Tahoe Valley. I was always overcome by the awesome majesty of the scene. Encircling my view, the mighty Sierra Nevada Mountains stood proudly, protecting the fragile alpine oasis from the merciless desert sands. Tall evergreens blanketed the feet of these rocky, snow-capped mountains as if cradling the lake and fertile valley away from the mountains' wind-swept harshness. Down below, surrounding the lake, the shoreline of massive granite boulders was occasionally broken by short stretches of white sand. Along the shore, small communities poked through the trees. Each had its own weathered, wooden boat docks jutting out into the cold, choppy water. Beyond the docks, from the unfathomable depths of the lake, the sun reflected a crystalline emerald color as brilliant and stunning as a flawless gem. The hypnotic effects were so powerful, sometimes it took the sharp sound of hammering or an electric saw to snap me from my blissful trance.

Although I had to wake up at five o'clock each morning to face another day of mentally and physically demanding labor, I generally had a good time. For example, the characters I worked with were very entertaining. Mike Swank, for instance, with his black beard and rough voice, looked and sounded exactly like the famous disc jockey, Wolfman Jack. Another crew member, Kinook, a wild and crazy French-Canadian, while riding in the back of a U-Haul truck delivering supplies, took off his clothes and started dancing around. The car behind us started to follow very closely, and the two ladies inside pointed, giggled, and appeared to enjoy the impromptu show. We were lucky we were not pulled over and arrested. One character, another which I doubt my mother would have approved of, was Mike Parker. He was proud of his personal record. He made sure that everyone knew that he was at one time a bouncer at a Nevada cat house. Also, he bragged that he had had various venereal diseases more often than he could count on both hands. I stayed away from him, not because of his past, but because he had the bad habit of shooting the nail gun at anyone within range. Everybody in the crew was unique—some maybe a bit more than others.

Even though the crew had its fun, we also took our work very seriously. Nothing was ever more gratifying to us than when we completed a project. One project we finished was a gorgeous, half-million dollar, Swiss-style mountain chalet. We knew we were a team, and were proud of what we had accomplished.

Obviously, my worst fears about the job proved to be unfounded. The cool, crisp mountain air had cleared my mind; the hard physical labor had toned my body; and the picturesque scenery and the colorful people became treasured memories. In fact, I had such an incredible experience that I returned to the same job for the next two summers.

Kevin's Comments

To write a composition about what I liked or disliked about one of my jobs was the topic assigned to my English class. I chose to write about my job at Lake Tahoe because the entire experience was so extraordinary and memorable that my other jobs seemed dull in comparison.

Although the memories were still vivid and quickly written into my rough draft, problems with geographical and chronological order caused the greatest frustrations. Some changes had to be made to assist the sentence transitions, but once I organized my thoughts, the writing went smoothly.

Nevertheless, the pleasure I had in recalling all the fond memories and reliving some of the same feelings did not equal the greater pleasure of sharing them with the people who read my paper.

CATHERINE SANDERS
Illinois State University
Jim Meyer, Instructor

Mom Had a Baby

Once I was the youngest child in my family. Now, I have a little sister. From the ages of zero to seven I was the baby and was very proud of this position, but as a belated birthday present Mom announced that she was pregnant, and my treasured status flew right out of the window. Anyone who was ever the baby for any length of time knows that there are great advantages to this job and at the tender age of seven to have these advantages not only taken away but passed on to someone else is heartbreaking. So there I was a spoiled, contented, master of all I surveyed, seven-year-old about to be dethroned, and I didn't like it one bit.

At first when Mom was pregnant, it was exciting to think I might have a little brother or sister, someone to push around and who would look up to me, but when Mom had the baby my whole way of life changed. The idea wasn't so exciting anymore. The household began to revolve around this one little person. People started saying, "Not now, Cookie, I'm feeding the baby" or "Don't mess with the baby, Cookie," and I couldn't handle it. This kid had her own room at the age of three days, and I was still sharing a room after seven years. If that wasn't bad enough, the family was making a fool of themselves over the kid. I'm talking cuchee coo and the whole works. Personally I didn't see what the fuss was about, the kid snored at 3 days old, a snore that would take most people years to develop. Everyone in the house thought this was just great, yet they got upset if I just breathed too loud.

My secret animosity lasted for a few months until one day I looked down at this perfect little human being with five fingers on every hand and five little toes on each foot and she grinned this silly toothless grin. To my surprise I found myself saying "cuchee coo" to this kid just like the rest of them. Before long I was begging to hold her, feed her, and even change her diapers. This kid who I thought was taking my place was instead making her own place in the family.

As ten-year-old Candy Charice Sanders will testify to, I now have come to deeply appreciate having a little sister to push around. I can't even imagine not having the little brat in the house. Just goes to show that first impressions aren't always correct.

Catherine's Comments

In class the teacher asked us to write as many sentences as possible with the form of "I once was _____ now I am _____." As I started writing sentences, many things came to mind. I didn't used to wear glasses but now I do, I used to have a short temper but now I don't, and I used to be the youngest but now I have a little sister. He then told us to pick a sentence and write a paper about it. I chose to do the paper about my little sister because I didn't think that the other sentences would be interesting stories.

The rough draft wasn't all that different from the final draft. Any changes that were made were basically phrases and punctuation rather than content. Writing the paper brought back many memories of things that I can laugh at now, but they weren't so funny then. Such as my jealousy of my sister in the beginning and my learning to cope with it.

HAKAN YALNIZ
Greenville Technical College (South Carolina)
Martha A. McWhite, Instructor

My First Trip to America

From the vantage point of my home country, Turkey, it looked very simple. I would board a plane in Instanbul, fly to Brussels, and after an overnight lay-over, fly to Newark and Charlotte. My American sponsor had made all the arrangements, sent me airline tickets, and a letter explaining the purpose and details of my journey. (Not that I could read the letter. After all, it was written in English.) Most importantly, I would be on my way to an American college education. Little did I realize that what I perceived as simply getting from point A to point B would turn into one of the most physically and emotionally uncomfortable experiences of my life.

Flying in the company of my countrymen from Istanbul gave me a false sense of security. I hit the language barrier with a crashing impact in the Brussels airport: Where was the hotel at which my sponsor had made reservations? After several torturous conversations in which my English-Turkish dictionary played a dominant role, I found the correct Holiday Inn. I was granted a short-lived reprieve when the desk clerk called in a Turkish hotel worker to assist in the check-in process. This is when I heard, in my native tongue, shocking news: The hotel expected money. I had understood a reservation to mean a room waiting and paid for. My sponsor had meant a room waiting only. My fear that I was being robbed was confirmed in the hotel dining room. I had asked the desk clerk to direct me to an inexpensive restaurant. Apparently, the words I selected from the dictionary had the opposite meaning. The language barrier continued to have a detrimental effect on my meals. My flight from Brussels to Newark was on People Express. (This is an airline which, if it were legal, would charge money to use the toilet.) I did not know the voice over the loudspeaker was referring to the lunch I expected to be served. I did not understand it to be saying that meals were not included in the price of a ticket. The engines hummed, and my stomach growled from Brussels to Newark.

I faced a three hour hurdle over the language barrier in the immigration office at the Newark Airport. Although I carried a five-year American student visa, the immigration officials didn't believe I was entering the country to study. The fact was that my English vocabulary consisted only of legitimate

American classroom material. They called my sponsor. He convinced them I was not a terrorist.

If the language I heard was strange, the appearance and behavior of some of the passengers I saw was even stranger. As I sat in my People Express seat, ten men boarded together and sat across the aisle from me. All ten men were dressed identically in black from hat to shoes. All carried black books, and all had long ringlets of hair hanging by their ears. They sat together, opened their books together, and read aloud together. I had heard of unusual religious cults in America. Would they speak to me, try to convert me, and take me to their commune? Another man sat close by. Although he was dressed more normally than that man in black, the fact that he was wearing earrings and makeup made me feel uncomfortable. He looked at me from time to time, making me afraid to close my eyes and sleep.

When I arrived in Charlotte, I was met by my sponsor and driven to his home in Greenville. He suggested I call my parents so they would know I had arrived safely. As we spoke, my father asked about my journey. My response was a lie. "Fine," I said. If he had asked me to return home on the next available flight, I may have told him the truth.

Hakan's Comments

When I wanted to write this essay, the first question that came in my mind was on which topic do I want to write? I was trying to find a most interesting subject. Two things came to my mind as a possible topic. The first one was my air travel from my country to America. The second one was, as a foreign student, what was my biggest problem in America. Finally I decided to write on my air travel because it wasn't a story people hear everyday. Since I started to learn English, my grammar has always been a problem. I have almost solved this problem by working with my teachers. When I want to write a paper, I spend a little more time than my American friends just to correct my grammar.

LARRY E. ENGLAND
State Technical Institute at Knoxville (Tennessee)
Eleanor R. Stiles, Instructor

There's One on Every Corner

"Suckers are a dime a dozen," my boss used to say. "They're like whores. There's one on every corner." He envisioned himself as a bird of prey, swooping in for the kill. I discovered a love/hate relationship growing between us. My boss was probably the most manipulative man I've ever known, and yet his financial genius was truly inspirational.

My boss was extraordinary in that he could manipulate anyone to do his bidding. He looked upon people as pathetic animals—sheep waiting to be fleeced. He even exploited his own family. Once, for instance, my boss was under investigation for siphoning off company funds. He forced his own son to take the blame by threatening to destroy the son's marriage with incriminating information he had acquired. In the end, my boss managed to maintain his control over the company while his son served time in jail for embezzlement. Predictably, the son's wife believed that her husband was guilty and filed for divorce. My boss had manipulated everyone.

In spite of his apparent need to manipulate people, my boss was a financial wizard at investments. He built an empire on hard work and determination. Sacrificing both his marriage and his health, he spent long hours buying and renovating old houses. Money became an obsession. He started buying apartment complexes all over the United States. Profits were flowing like rivers, circulating faster and faster. His next step was the purchase of a major chain of nursing homes and convalescent hospitals. With most of his financial empire now located in the western part of the United States, my boss relocated his company headquarters to Los Angeles. Simultaneously, disaster struck. Apartment complexes in Oklahoma were lost due to floods. Dallas holdings were destroyed by fire. The dream was over. In his intoxicating obsession to obtain wealth, my boss had inadequately insured his properties.

Today, my ex-boss controls only a tiny part of what was once a tremendously powerful empire. He's lost his family, his friends, and his wealth. The manipulator has finally been manipulated. There's one on every corner.

Larry's Comments

My first consideration in writing this composition was to find a subject with a personality so strong and domineering that everyone could relate to him. I chose my ex-boss because of the inspiration he had made on my life, which dramatically changed my way of thinking forever. I felt that most readers could identify someone in their own lives who has possessed the traits I was describing, thus enabling me to communicate my feelings more successfully.

In writing my composition, I found the greatest problem I encountered was in trying to remain objective. I made several changes in my rough drafts, attempting to communicate only the methods of my subject's ambitions, and not my personal opinion of his methods. My greatest reward came when I showed my composition to others who had known my ex-boss. My friends said I had captured the man perfectly.

JUDITH DE GROAT
Merrit College (California)
Renata Polt Schmitt, Instructor

Look What's Happened to Christmas

How sad it is that the true meaning of Christmas seems to have gotten lost somewhere between Macy's and Toys R Us. Children believe in Mom, Dad, and Master Charge, not Santa. Their definition of Christmas is very simple; it's the day their parents give the biggest, baddest whatever gift on their block. Most children know long before Christmas what to expect under the tree. Why? Because Mom and Pop took them shopping. What better way to save time, eliminate guesswork, returns and please everyone at the same time?

Grandma has an artificial tree, buys her cookies and fruit and nutbreads from her favorite bakery. She desires a Gucci handbag, a pair of Guess jeans and a microwave from the grandchildren for Christmas, and expects to get it.

Christmas caroling is too corny, designer stockings are in and it's just too cool to attend church on Christmas Eve or Christmas Day. The element of surprise on Christmas morning went out with 78 RPM records. The average department store Santa looks to be about 21 years of age, on a hunger strike and he never says, "Ho, Ho, Ho!"

I predict that in the near future a revision of our outdated traditional Christmas carols is next on the agenda and "Jingle Bells" will go something like this:

> *Dashing through the malls*
> *To catch the sales each day,*
> *As cheap as it may be*
> *Still can't afford to pay.*
> *So over our heads we'll go*
> *And sign our lives away.*
> *What fun to shop for family and friends*
> *To make their Christmas gay!*
>
> *Jingle bells, Christmas sales,*
> *Use credit cards all the way!*
> *Oh what fun it is to charge*
> *And bring gifts home today.*
> *(repeat chorus)*

All I can say is "Help!" Christmas has become nothing more than a field day for department stores, and most of us have fallen into the commercial trap. We are robbing our children of the real joy of Christmas and the true meaning it holds. Christmas should be a memorable, not profitable, experience. If we can restore old Victorian homes, trolley cars and the Statue of Liberty, etc., then surely we can restore something as simple as Christmas to the beautiful holiday it once was.

Judith's Comments

I was notified approximately two and a half weeks before Christmas about the essay contest. I wondered if I would have enough time to do a paper and send it in by the due date. I was in the midst of tackling my Christmas shopping, baking, wrapping, etc. It then became apparent to me that Christmas would be an ideal topic for an essay at this time, and I proceeded to follow through with the contest.

As my essay was coming along, I realized how fortunate I was as a youngster to have experienced Christmas the way it should be as opposed to how it is celebrated now. I hadn't realized how drastically Christmas had changed until I wrote this essay.

DISCOVERY

DANIEL LUTHER
Youngstown State University (Ohio)
Margaret Ridge, Instructor

Pre-Realization

There's two down, nobody on, no score, the bottom of the ninth. The batter steps to the plate staring at the sheer intensity in the pitcher's eye. Strike one! The crowd falls completely silent. The southpaw knuckleballer delivers a second offering. Swing and a miss!! The batter steps out of his box, sighs deeply, and resumes his stance. The man on the mound tosses his bread-and-butter pitch. Crack! The ball flies deep into centerfield. It's going! The outfielder drops back to the wall. It's going! The whole universe watches both the ball drifting and the lunging outfielder extend his glove further than what seems possible. It's going to be close!

For a split second, both teams, all of the fans, the umpires, and everyone else involved, pre-empts every other emotion and puts all sense of reality on stand by for what I have termed as "pre-realization."

During the brief instant of "pre-realization," a variety of other emotions are simultaneously felt in perfect unison. In our case, there is a great deal of suspense felt from the moment the pitch was hit. A feeling of worry arose when it was realized that the ball might be caught. Anticipation comes into play when the batter approaches the box. Hope is felt with the beginning of the inning. And excitement has been the story of the whole game. All five of these emotions are felt in different degrees throughout the game. They all climax for a split second in equal intensity just before the ball either lands over the fence or is caught. This is the split second of "pre-realization."

Remember when you were a kid? For weeks you waited for Christmas day. After Santa did finally come, you woke up hours before the sun came up and stared at all of the packages. After dragging everyone out of bed at some ungodly hour, you planted yourself in the middle of the packaged presents. With an "O.K." from mom, you tore the wrapping off of the closest present. The instant after all of the paper was off, but before your eyes focused on exactly what was unwrapped, the feeling of "pre-realization" was felt.

This emotion is not limited to sporting events and gift-receiving. It could be found in mystery novels just before it is announced that the butler did it. Or on a rollercoaster when you finally reach the top and peer down. As you lean back on two legs of a chair, it is felt just before you reach out and save yourself from falling.

If what is known—what is happening—what is now—can be represented by a door and what is unknown—what is the outcome—what is to be—can be represented by what is beyond the door, then "pre-realization" is the archway between.

"Pre-realization" is not excitement because it also has elements of depression involved. ("What if the ball is caught?") It is not hope because that is counter-balanced by dismay. It is not anticipation because waiting is at its end. It is not doubt because the answer will all too soon be evident. It is not adventure because the adventure continues.

"Pre-realization" is all of these and none of these. It is a paradoxical array of completely mixed emotions at their ultimate, equilibrant climax.

Daniel's Comments

I wrote the "Pre-realization" essay in response to a writing assignment which was to write an essay on an abstract term. We were given one week to compose it. For the first three days, I did not take pen in hand. I bounced various abstract terms around in my head searching for the one I could write on. On the fourth day and after an exhaustive nine hour shift at a "Hardee's" Restaurant, I sat back in my office chair waiting for the other closers to finish their work. I leaned back on the chair and almost fell! I sat up and feverishly began writing what emotions just passed through my mind—anticipation—worry—fear—excitement. I then coined the term "Pre-realization."

The fifth day I began defining it with: a) a cliff-hanging opening example; b) an analysis of that example; c) a brief example almost anyone could relate to; d) several other examples showing that the emotion is felt everywhere; e) a metaphor; f) a second analysis of what it isn't; and g) a closing containing the definition of the word. On the sixth day I revised the essay, corrected the spelling errors and punctuation.

On the seventh day I handed it in.

JANINE BLANK
State Technical Institute at Knoxville (Tennessee)
Eleanor R. Stiles, Instructor

Learning from Apes

Throughout the years, man has sought ways to communicate with the animal world. Although television sitcoms have depicted animals such as horses and dogs as rational, speaking creatures with human qualities, the ape family, having similar body chemistry and brain structure to humans, has been of most interest. Research studies dealing with ape language development have shown remarkable results and offer hopeful applications for the future.

For nine months beginning in June 1931, Professor and Mrs. W.N. Kellogg of Indiana University conducted a study to compare the similarities and differences in basic skills development between a 7 1/2 month old chimpanzee, Gua, and their ten-month-old son, Donald. Each was cared for in the Kellogg home, being exposed to the same daily routine and training. Comparisons were made of the ape's and child's physical strength, as well as their manual skill, memory, recognition, and language development. Although there are definite limitations to an ape's ability to adapt to human society, the ape and child, in spite of displaying some differences, were remarkably similar in many ways. For example, Gua was superior in motor dexterity, while Donald showed steady advances in more precise tactile and manual dexterity. Observations of their play life showed likeness, yet Donald displayed superiority in his tendency to explore and manipulate his environment. Differences in social reactiveness were evidenced in Donald's bashfulness, revealing "an emerging sense of self" (Young 10); however, Gua never did develop such an attitude. Gessell intelligence tests revealed that the learning of the two was closely paralleled (Young 8–11).

On the other hand, Donald was clearly superior in vocal communication. Though at first Gua learned to correctly respond to human commands, the child later surpassed the ape in verbal comprehension. Moreover, while similar care and training were given to both the ape and child, Gua never "acquired a single human word" (Young 11).

Young summarized the results of the Kellogg study as follows:

There is little doubt that had the ape remained in the Kellogg home, her human companion would soon have outstripped her in acquiring the essential qualities of communication and conduct which so sharply distinguish the socialized homo sapiens *from the anthropoid. These include such items as true language and the use of concepts, memory couched in symbolic form, the skilled use of tools and other material objects, and above all else the qualities which we call human personality. (11)*

However, later studies have revealed new findings. Isaac Asimov wrote in *Science Digest* that although physically the larger primates have much in common with human beings, the greatest difference between the two species is in the size of the brain. The chimpanzee's brain, unlike the human brain, has not developed a portion of itself called *Broca's convolution,* which controls the muscles that make speech possible. Asimov also reported that although "the chimpanzee lacks Broca's convolution . . . it may have the germs of communication" (89). Asimov also asserted that contrary to the belief that only man can show rationality, chimpanzees have been taught gestures to carry on simple, yet rational, conversations with human beings (88–89).

In fact, at Emory University's Yerkes Regional Primate Center computers have been developed to teach chimpanzees "to read and write in a brand new language called Yerkish." The different keys on the console are geometric forms, and by pressing the keys, symbols are reproduced on a teleprinter as the words they represent. In this way, a form of non-verbal "conversation" can be carried on with chimpanzees. Consequently, scientists at the research center taught Yerkish to a three-year-old chimpanzee named Lana. Using a Yerkish keyboard, Lana first learned to make simple requests for her favorite foods. Later, as the scientists required her to hit the key in proper sequence to receive her treat, Lana learned to form complete sentences. She also learned to recognize symbols on the screen and differentiate between a correct sentence and an incorrect one. In other words, Lana appeared to "read" the symbols on the screen. Scientists hope to see increased vocabulary in Lana in the future ("Lessons").

Another example of a chimpanzee's using the Yerkish language is a four-year-old chimp named Kanzi. As reported in "Chimp Learning Language Skills," a June 1985 newspaper article, Kanzi "has demonstrated the most human-like linguistic skills ever documented in another animal" (9).

Besides Yerkish, studies have also been done with gorillas and sign language. Psychologist Francine "Penny" Patterson has been experimenting with teaching sign language to a pair of gorillas, Koko, from the San Francisco Zoo, and Michael, whom she acquired later. When the experiment began in 1972, Patterson started teaching Koko American Sign Language (Amesian). After moving to Stanford and acquiring Michael, Patterson eventually moved with her gorillas to a private site outside of San Francisco to tutor her students further. Results of her experiments with the gorillas have shown that they use sign language "spontaneously and appropriately," not only to their instructors and reporters, but to each other as well (Logan 58). Further evidence of rational thought was shown when Koko asked for a kitten and was given a tailless Manx, which later died. Once told of the kitten's death, Koko showed signs of sadness. Moreover, as human-like as Koko seems, even she can distinguish a human from an animal. For example, when asked in which category she belonged, Koko replied, "Fine animal gorilla" (Logan 60). However, some scientists, including Thomas Seboek, a linguistics expert and professor at Indiana University, dispute the idea that Koko functions rationally. "There are absolutely no species besides humans," Seboek says, "who have language capability" (Logan 60).

However, teaching apes methods of non-verbal communication has been only the beginning. If apes can be taught to communicate non-verbally, perhaps this approach can be used to help youngsters with language difficulties. At the same time, perhaps real communication with the animal world can become a reality. "Wouldn't you like to know what a chimp thinks about?" says Georgia State University Psychologist Duane M. Rumbaugh. "Perhaps one day Lana or another chimp can act as an interpreter between their world and ours" ("Lessons").

One current way in which the results of ape language studies are being used is at the Developmental Learning Center at Atlanta's Georgia Regional Hospital where the Yerkish language is successfully being taught to mentally retarded patients who formerly were unable to communicate at all. According to Steve Watson, director at the center, studies have shown great progress. For the retarded, having a way to communicate is " . . . a way of being set free." Now that the patients have learned to express their wants and needs, they have experienced a lower rate of temper tantrums. Hopes that the retarded can lead a more normal life are being realized. Additionally, in the Clayton County, Georgia, public schools, retarded students have also been introduced to Yerkish, and scientists, through their research with apes, hope to get a better understanding of what causes language difficulties. Meanwhile, Rumbaugh "hopes . . . a lightweight, economical version of the Yerkish keyboard . . . will be developed to aid the speech impaired in homes and schools" (Kerjoda and Carroll 66).

Through man's eagerness to communicate with the animal world, he has accomplished feats never before dreamed possible. Research has shown great progress in non-verbal communication, and there remain untold implications for the future. Perhaps one day man can further understand the animal world, and the communication barrier between humans and their fellow creatures can be broken.

Works Cited

Asimov, Isaac. "Chimps Tell Us About Evolution." *Science Digest*, November 1964: 88–89.

"Chimp Learning Language Skills." *The Daily Times* [Maryville, TN] 24 June 1985: 9.

Kerjoda, Eileen, and Ginny Carroll. "Scaling the Walls of Silence." *Newsweek* 8 July 1985: 66.

"Lessons for Lana." *Time* 4 March 1974: 74.

Logan, Marcia. "Koko, the Talking Gorilla, Gets a Brand-New Kitty, and Primate Fans the World Over Go Ape." *People* 22 April 1985: 57–60.

Young, Kimball. *Sociology*. New York: American Book Company, 1942.

Janine's Comments

The topic of ape language was chosen in class for an assignment to write a research paper. The rough draft of the paper was to be written and submitted in three parts. These three parts were then revised and compiled into a final copy.

There were many changes made from draft to draft. First, while reading through the material, I made rough sentence outlines from the information about the topic and then formed this rough outline into paragraphs. I also rephrased the material from draft to draft and reconstructed sentences. Last, the information was organized into the proper time sequence.

One of the major problems encountered in writing my research paper was keeping closely to the thesis. Paraphrasing and choosing the most important quotes also posed some problems. It was also difficult, I felt, to create an interest in the readers' minds.

One of the rewards in writing my research paper was seeing the three parts put together into a final revision. Also, having my paper submitted for this essay contest is most rewarding.

Index